NOTICE

NO ADMITTANCE
EXCEPT
ON PLEASURE

WHEN GRANDMAMA FELL OFF THE BOAT

THE BEST OF
HARRY GRAHAM

INVENTOR OF
RUTHLESS RHYMES

WITH AN INTRODUCTION BY
MILES KINGTON

METHUEN

A METHUEN HUMOUR CLASSIC

This collection first published in 1986
by Methuen London Ltd
11 New Fetter Lane, London EC4P 4EE

Conceived, designed and produced
by Sheldrake Press Ltd
188 Cavendish Road, London SW12 0DA
© 1986 Sheldrake Publishing Ltd
Verses © V. Thesiger

Sheldrake Press Ltd would like to thank John Ince
and Karin B. Hills for their invaluable help in
the compilation of this volume.

British Library Cataloguing in Publication Data
Graham, Harry, *1874-1936*
    When Grandmama fell off the boat: the best of Harry Graham
    I. Title
    821'.8   PR6013.R18
    ISBN 0-413-14160-8

Typeset by SX Composing Ltd
Printed in Hong Kong by Imago Publishing Ltd

— FOREWORD —

ON reading these verses, most of which are in the worst possible taste and would nowadays be termed "sick", it is hard to believe that their author was the most gentle and amiable man imaginable. Obviously, underlying his good nature there was a streak of cynicism, and yet I never saw my father cross nor heard him being sarcastic or unkind. This may possibly have been because he was by temperament lazy, and like most lazy people he could not be bothered, even if he felt like it, to be annoyed about anything: and yet it is more probable that his tolerance and affability stemmed from his belief in man's innate absurdity. His mockery lacked malice since he could not help seeing the human race as droll rather than wicked.

As a father he was perfect. Not only did he make exquisite puns and playful allusions – such as writing of a tennis player "she also served but mostly stood and waited" – but he had the gift, which I appreciated when I was small, of being thoroughly silly.

He died when I was twenty-five, which is a very long time ago, but I can still see him, looking very much the Guards officer he was, sitting at his writing table (in clouds of smoke, alas), covering pages of foolscap with increasingly squiggly writing in his search for the perfect rhyme, the exactly right word. For where writing was concerned he was a perfectionist, and "June" never had rhymed and never would rhyme with "tune".

In the following pages there are many of these words, which will still, I hope, induce the laughter that enveloped so much of my youth.

VIRGINIA GRAHAM

LONDON 1986

— INTRODUCTION —

MY father was not a great collector of poetry. The fact that he had several volumes of Robert Graves on his shelves came, I think, more from the fact that his old regiment, the Royal Welch Fusiliers, was also Robert Graves's old regiment than from any inherent love of verse. So where his copy of *Ruthless Rhymes for Heartless Homes* came from I do not know, especially as Harry Graham was in the Coldstream Guards, but there it was on the shelves one day, and when I found it as a young boy I knew I had come upon a masterpiece.

The title *Ruthless Rhymes* is itself a stroke of genius. It announces exactly the streak of anti-sentimental, murderous warmth that runs through them. Few are more than four lines long, yet in each one Graham manages to include a violent accident or act of assault which usually leads to instant death. It contains more corpses than an Ed McBain thriller and more viciousness than a volume of the Marquis de Sade. It must, in fact, be one of the most violent books ever published. It is also one of the funniest, and one of the best written. Its combination of light-heartedness and callousness appealed to me enormously at fourteen, which is a light-hearted and callous age, but thirty years on I find them as wonderful as ever. Either I have failed to grow up properly, or Harry Graham wrote a classic. I think both, probably.

From time to time in these thirty years I have wondered what else Harry Graham wrote, and indeed who he was, and writing this introduction has given me the treat of finding out both. The surprise is that he was born to be a pillar of the Establishment. His father was Sir Henry Graham, a barrister, and his mother was the daughter of the Earl of Cranbrook. His elder brother, Sir Ronald, was a Foreign Office dignitary (British Ambassador to Rome in 1921), and Harry too might have gone on to diplomacy and a knighthood if the profits and delights of the pen had not proved stronger.

Born in 1874, two days before Christmas, he went to Eton, Sandhurst and the Coldstream Guards, and after three years in the latter establishment found himself appointed aide-de-camp to the new Governor-General of Canada, Lord Minto. Apart from a two-year gap on active service in the Boer War, he stayed with Lord Minto from 1898 to 1904. A dull and serious business it might have seemed, but Lord Minto's letters to his wife prove otherwise: "Harry quite awful and makes me hysterical, he is so amusing," he reports. When he left, Lord Minto wrote: "I miss Harry very much – he loves all the girls and they all love him . . . he is an excellent and a most amusing companion."

As an ADC he must have been efficient to be kept on for six years, though not super-efficient. Minto again: "Fancy that idiot Harry Graham has lost all the things I gave him to take to England – my skating boots, skates and things for Mathews – it is maddening. I hope from his letter he has made some mistake . . . but I always say, the brain of an ADC is an awful thing." Still, Graham did make a success of organising such undertakings as an arduous journey to the Klondyke in 1900; he wrote an account of the trip which he presented to Lord Minto, and which has since resurfaced from a Canadian publisher under the title *Across Canada to the Klondyke*.

But that was not the first thing he wrote. In 1899 he had published *Ruthless Rhymes for Heartless Homes*, under the pseudonym of Col. D. Streamer, and it must have been the success of this and subsequent volumes of verse which gradually lured him away from official life. In 1904 he resigned from the army to become private secretary to Lord Roseberry.

Graham stayed with Lord Roseberry for two years, during which time he became engaged to the American actress Ethel Barrymore. Although they even got as far as buying a house together in London, it never led to marriage. In 1906 he severed all links with Miss Barrymore, Lord Roseberry and official life, and became a full-time writer until his death in 1936. He wrote stories, he wrote volumes of verse, he wrote lyrics for musicals and plays, and he often had three or four productions running in the West End at the same time. In 1931 he adapted *The White Horse Inn* from the original German, and it ran for 651 performances. Meanwhile he had married Dorothy Villiers in 1910 and had one daughter, Virginia, a gifted writer herself and a long-time contributor to *Punch*. Graham did not like publicity about himself, and was delighted that the only photograph of him, with his daughter, that ever appeared in the gossip magazines was captioned: "Miss Graham and friend."

And yet, after this highly successful career, the only works of Harry Graham that remain in print are the original *Ruthless Rhymes* and *More Ruthless Rhymes* (1930). Gavin Ewart, another fine verse writer, published a piece on Harry Graham in the *London Magazine* in 1964 in which he suggested that nothing else Graham wrote was half as good as his *Ruthless Rhymes*. This is a harsh judgement which he implicitly takes back by quoting reams of stuff from other volumes. I think it would be truer to say that no other *book* Graham wrote was as comprehensively satisfying as the two *Ruthless Rhymes* volumes, but that they all contained material that was quite as good. "Mrs Christopher Columbus" is the best poem ever written on the advantages of an absentee husband, and I think that "The Bath" is better than anything in *Ruthless Rhymes*, although Gavin Ewart does not even mention it.

What is needed, in fact, is a book that gathers together all the best of Harry Graham's verse from the turn of the century to 1936 – and that, by a strange coincidence, is exactly what this book does. Considering that Britain has always loved its light verse writers, and produced some of the best, such as Lear, Gilbert and Belloc, it is strange that we have forgotten one of the finest of all – immeasurably better than Belloc, says Ewart. Graham gave light verse a cutting edge which it seldom possesses; his playfulness always has a sting in the tail. We tend to think of the Edwardian age as being rather soft and plump, but it did contain a streak of wickedness which we would do very well to envy. One only has to think of Saki's short stories to see the same steely suaveness in operation, or, in a different sphere, E. F. Benson's "Mapp and Lucia" stories. Benson and Saki have recently found favour again, and it is high time that Harry Graham received his due.

Just how far he has receded in the public memory is illustrated by, of all people, the late Agatha Christie. I have a friend in New York called Babette Rosmond who once wrote to the Dame to enquire about four lines of poetry quoted by one of her characters:

> The days passed slowly, one by one;
> I fed the ducks, reproved my wife,
> Played Handel's *Largo* on the fife,
> Or gave the dog a run.

Had Agatha Christie written these lines herself, my friend wanted to know, and if not, who had? Agatha Christie wrote back to say she had not written them, and she could not remember the true author. My friend subsequently wrote to everyone she could think of, and not one person even recognized the lines, except the crime writer and novelist Ruth Rendell – and she could not for the life of her remember who wrote them. So you can imagine the start of delight I gave when I discovered on page 104 of this book a poem called "Creature Comforts", with those very same lines embedded in the first verse. The news, alas, has come too late for Agatha Christie, but not for the rest of us.

When Harry Graham died, *The Times* devoted a leading article to him in which it was said that he pushed through satire and came out on the other side into a kingdom of nonsense all his own. Edward Lear was "Graham's only possible companion in a world which would have seemed too irresponsible to either Lewis Carroll or Gilbert." I agree with every word of it. But the customary period of neglect following a *Times* obituary has gone on for far too long. It is time now for the revival to begin.

MILES KINGTON

LONDON 1986

— INDIFFERENCE —

WHEN Grandmama fell off the boat,
  And couldn't swim (and wouldn't float),
Matilda just stood by and smiled.
I almost could have slapped the child.

— APPRECIATION —

AUNTIE, did you feel no pain
Falling from that willow tree?
Will you do it, please, again?
'Cos my friend here didn't see.

— FATHER —

DURING dinner at the Ritz,
Father kept on having fits,
And, which made my sorrow greater,
I was left to tip the waiter.

— AUNT ELIZA —

IN the drinking-well
Which the plumber built her,
Aunt Eliza fell...

We must buy a filter.

— AMIABILITY —

HOW fond I was of Uncle Dan;
Not since creation first began
Was there a more good-natured man,
    More kindly or indulgent.
His ample face (he weighed a ton)
On ev'rything and ev'ry one
Shone like some vast, benignant sun,
    As warm and as effulgent –
A simple soul, devoid of guile,
His life was one unending smile.

He never lost his self-control
At golf when, at the eighteenth hole,
His "putt" was bunkered by a mole,
    Or he was laid a "stymie";
He never got the least annoyed
When children (semi-anthropoid)
His priceless ornaments destroyed
    Or made his shirt-front grimy;
At bridge he took it as a joke
If partners happened to revoke.

I still remember how he smiled
When Gwendolen, his only child,
Was by a foreigner beguiled
    And afterwards deserted;
And when his youngest nephew, Phil,
Who forged his name upon a bill,
Presented it with cunning skill,
    And into cash converted,
A smile my uncle's face o'erspread:
"Boys will be boys!" was all he said.

And when his wife eloped one day,
Because she could no longer stay
With one who never would display
    The slightest sign of temper,
More wide my uncle's grins became,
He uttered not a word of blame,
His motto still remained the same:
    "Still smiling" ("*Ridens semper*").

He helped his erring spouse to pack,
And, later on, he took her back.

At last his friends could bear no more.
They led him to the mad-house door,
Where he, poor soul! to swell the score
   Of demi-wits was added.
Such trials he was still above;
"Strait-waistcoats," he remarked, "I love;
They really fit one like a glove;
   How well this cell is padded!
Cocaine is a delightful drug!
This water-bed is nice and snug!"

Moral
Though hearts by kindliness are won,
Good-nature can be overdone;
Excessive smiling we should shun,
    Such sweetness can be cloying;
And men who, when our temper's short,
Decline to quarrel or show sport,
But still with courtesy retort,
    Are terribly annoying.
A healthy grumble, now and then,
Is good for women and for men.

THE NEW
— PROFESSION —

MY scatterbrained nephew gave such an
    impression
  Of being inept and half-witted,
He never was able to find a profession
    For which he was properly fitted.
He's failed seven times for the Army, so far,
    And his tutor, in language emphatic,
Declares that he hasn't the brains for the Bar
    Nor the *nous* for the Corps Diplomatic.
This morning, however, my witless relation
Discovered at last a becoming vocation.

The work, so he tells me, is easy and pleasant,
    The hours are too short to be wearing,
And a man can contrive to be "Absent yet
    Present,"
    By means of a system called "pairing,"
At ease he may loll on a bench, half-awake,
    While a colleague is airing some hobby,
Or the gentlest description of exercise take
    In a place that is known as the Lobby,
Receiving four hundred a year compensation,
As well as a probable six months' vacation.

Rejoice, then, ye fathers, rejoice beyond measure!
    Be thankful, ye sisters and mothers!
The chance of employment, with profit and
        pleasure,
    Has come to your sons and your brothers!
How gladly they add such a splendid career
    To the list of the open professions,
How bright are the thoughts of four hundred a
        year
    That illumine their facial expressions!
They gaze at the House with redoubled affection,
And oh! how they long for a Gen'ral Election!

— THOUGHTLESSNESS —

I NEVER shall forget my shame
To find my son had forged my name.
If he'd had any thought for others
He might at least have forged his mother's.

— GRANDPAPA —

MY dining-room is large and light
(Twelve feet by nine, or very nearly),
And on its walls, both left and right,
"Old Masters" hang, at ev'ry height,
  Where all may see them clearly:
Dangling from their respective wires,
The fam'ly portraits of my sires.

Great-uncle Charles, in gold and blue
  (A second Nelson he was reckoned),
And Great-aunt Arabella, too,
Who, if what Greville says is true,
  Was loved by George the Second;
And that stout ancestor, Sir Carey,
Who made such play with Bloody Mary.

Here, too, are prints of Speaker Strouchan*
  Whose rulings flowed like molten lava,
Of Bertram, thirteenth Baron Bolquhoun,†
Of Admiral Sir Maurice Moynigan‡
  Who fell at Balaclava,
Of Bishop Waughan,§ that great divine –
All famous ancestors of mine.

Upon an easel, too, observe
  The portrait that so proudly stands here
Instinct in ev'ry line and curve
With all the charm, the grace, the verve
  Of good Sir Edwin Landseer,
An artist who was quite the rage
In Queen Victoria's spacious age.

*Pronounced "Stroon." ‡Pronounced "Moon."
†Pronounced "Boon." §Pronounced "Woon."

No picture this of hinds at play,
    Of mongrels that with mastiffs quarrel,
Of Shetland ponies munching hay,
Of Monarchs of the Glen at Bay
    In marshes near Balmoral,
Or dachshunds (of the slim and wan sort)
Retrieving grouse for the Prince Consort.

Inspect this subject well, and note
    The whiskers centrally divided,
The silken stock about his throat,
The loose but elegant frock-coat,
    The boots (elastic-sided),
And you'll at once remark: "Ah, ha!
This must, of course, be Grandpapa!"

A model English squire, 'twas he
   Who entertained the local gentry;
Though not himself at home for tea,
To his demesne a paltry fee
   Of sixpence gave them entry,
And through his grounds they all might pass,
Though cautioned to KEEP OFF THE GRASS.

The Park was free on Saturdays.
   Here members of the lower orders
Could watch my grandsire's cattle graze
Or (through their op'ra-glasses) gaze
   At his herbaceous borders.
The masses he most truly pitied,
Though BICYCLISTS were NOT ADMITTED.

As yet upon his vast estates
   No labour troubles had arisen;
There were no beggars at his gates –
He and his brother-magistrates
   Had sent them all to prison,
Knowing 'twas wiser to avoid
Encouraging the Unemployed.

Though tender-hearted, I declare,
   And often moved to righteous rages
When told that his own workmen were
Reduced to vegetarian fare
   By their starvation wages,
Such gloomy topics he'd dismiss –
He knew there was no cure for this.

But if a villager fell sick
   He'd send the invalid a rabbit;
When lightning struck a yeoman's rick
'Twould cut him to the very quick,
   He'd sigh: "Poor Farmer Crabbett!
He'll have no fodder for his cow;
I'd best foreclose the mortgage now!"

In politics it was his rule
   To be broadminded but despotic;
In argument he kept quite cool,
Knowing a man to be a fool
   And most unpatriotic
Who differed from the views that he
Had cherished from the age of three.

Once I recall – a sad affair –
   When, as a child of years still tender,
I chanced to sit in *his* armchair,
He seized me roughly by the hair
   And flung me in the fender.
He had such quaint impulsive ways;
I didn't sit again for days.

Dear Grandpapa – I see him yet,
   My friend, philosopher and guide, too,
A personality, once met,
One could not possibly forget,
   Though lots of people tried to –
Founder of a distinguished line,
And worthy ancestor of mine!

TENDER-
— HEARTEDNESS —

BILLY, in one of his nice new sashes,
Fell in the fire and was burnt to ashes;
Now, although the room grows chilly,
I haven't the heart to poke poor Billy.

— MR JONES —

"THERE'S been an accident!" they said,
  "Your servant's cut in half; he's dead!"
"Indeed!" said Mr Jones, "and please
Send me the half that's got my keys."

— COMPENSATION —

WEEP not for little Léonie,
  Abducted by a French *Marquis*!
Though loss of honour was a wrench,
Just think how it's improved her French!

— THE LINGUIST —

During the German Emperor's recent visit to Brussels Baron
de Haulleville, Director of the Congo Museum, was
presented to His Majesty. The Kaiser "spoke at length with
the Baron in French, German, and English," says the *Daily
Mail.*

"GUTEN Morgen, mon ami!
Heute ist es schönes Wetter!
Charmé de vous voir içi!
    Never saw you looking better!"

"Hoffentlich que la Baronne,
    So entzuckend et so pleasant,
Ist in Brussels cet automne.
    Combien wunsch'ich she were present!"

"Und die kinder, how are they?
    Ont ils eu la rougeole lately?
Sind sie avec vous to-day?
    J'aimerais les treffen greatly."

"Ich muss chercher mon hotel.
    What a charming schwätzerei, sir!
Lebe wohl! Adieu! Farewell!
    Vive le Congo! Hoch der Kaiser!"

— THE SIREN —

'MID summertime's fantastic heat,
When urban pavements parch the feet,
To some far loophole of retreat
    Our drowsy thoughts go straying;
In bondage on each office-stool,
We dream of caverns dim and cool,
Of shady grots beside some pool
    Where nymphs and fauns are playing,
Where timid dryads coyly scatter
In flight before the local satyr.

While some (the more romantic chaps)
May plan a walking-tour, perhaps,
Where coloured counties spread their maps
    For Shropshire lads on Bredon,
And some (the richer fellows) plot
A cruise to Lapland in a yacht,
And thus enjoy, if polyglot,
    The voice that breathes o'er Sweden,
And others yearn for Monte Carlo,
For Fontainebleau, or even Marlow,

Much simpler travel-tastes have I;
My needs the humblest joys supply;
I never try to aim too high,
    Nor choose too large a target,
For I recall (sweet souvenir!)
The holiday I spent, last year,
In seaside lodgings with my dear
    Aunt Ramsgaret at Margate,*
With whom and where that blest vacation
Was one long round of dissipation.

*Should this not be "Aunt Margaret at Ramsgate"? – *Pub.*
Yes. – *H.G.*

28

Each morning she would take the air,
Propelled by me in a bath-chair –
That is, the weather being fair
    And other things propitious.
Then home to lunch we gaily hied,
And though, I own, the meal supplied
Erred somewhat on the frugal side,
    The mince was quite delicious,
And tapioca, too, would follow,
With lumps that were sheer joy to swallow.

Sea-bathing was a sport I'd planned,
But the authorities had banned
Undressing on the open strand,
    And though a Nature-lover
Might deem such regulations strange,
They would not suffer a sea-change
Unless one somehow could arrange
    To do it under cover;
Attempts to shed one's underclothing
In public they beheld with loathing.

Though this was something of a blow,
My habits I would not forgo –
*"Aut nec aut nihil,"** as you know,
    Has always been my motto –
And, after tea, when Auntie lay
Upon her couch, I'd slip away
To a sequestered little bay
    Where (in a cave or grotto)
My garments' plenary removal
Could meet with no one's disapproval.

*"Neck or nothing."

One evening, as I doffed my socks,
I noticed here upon the rocks
A maiden with peroxide locks
    Who sat and watched me stripping.
She wore a one-piece bathing-suit
And was a most attractive "beaut,"
And when she said: "Hullo, old fruit!"
    I felt that I was slipping.
And when she giggled rather sweetly
I knew that I had fall'n completely!

Then up she sprang and, like a shot,
(She was a lovesome thing, God wot!)
She bolted from that cave or grot
    And leapt into the briny.
She sank like – was it Milton said? –
A daystar in the ocean bed,
Then reared anon her dripping head
    As, with her eyes all shiny,
She shouted: "Catch me if you can, sir!"
And dived again like a merganser!

A moment's start was all I gave,
Then darted from my grot or cave,
And through the cool translucent wave
    Pursued the nymph and caught her;
In vain she struggled to escape;
I seized her firmly by the nape
(Which was of most convenient shape)
    And home rejoicing brought her.
"Oh, fie!" she cried, "You didn't otto!"
But "Neck or nothing" – that's my motto!

'Twas thus our love-affair began.
Each day, as to that cave I ran,
The offing for her form I'd scan,
    I couldn't live without it!
She looked so sweet in deshabille,
And when she kept an even keel
She seemed as graceful as a seal –
    I spoke to her about it.
She answered: "What of *your* vile *corpus*?
No doubt 'twas made like that on porpoise!"

Ah, yes, she'd such a sense of fun,
She dearly loved a harmless pun;
I well remember making one
   That specially rejoiced her.
As we were swimming through a shoal,
I murmured: "There's no plaice like sole!"
And on a breakwater (or mole)
   Suggested I should "'oist-'er!"
She smiled a smile so quaint, so elfish,
And said: "That would be very shellfish!"

Such happiness was doomed, alas!
My Aunt, to watch *The Skylark* pass,
One evening, through her op'ra-glass
   Quite innocently gazing,
Observed us sporting in the foam;
Her colour changed from puce to chrome,
She hurried forth and dragged me home,
   Her eyes with anger blazing,
And packed me off, next morning early,
To "Kenilworth," my home near Purley.

*

I've never met my Siren since,
And yet, whenever I eat mince
Or tapioca, I evince
   Strong symptoms of emotion.
In retrospect I see her still,
Broadbased upon that rocky sill,
Submerged or compassed (as you will)
   By the inviolate ocean!
And distance does but serve to heighten
The mem'ry of our time at Brighton!*

*Should this not be "Margate"? – *Ed.*
  No. Ramsgate. – *H.G.*

— PATIENCE —

WHEN skiing in the Engadine
My hat blew off down a ravine.
My son, who went to fetch it back,
Slipped through an icy glacier's crack
And then got permanently stuck.
It really was infernal luck:
My hat was practically new –
I loved my little Henry too –
And I may have to wait for years
Till either of them reappears.

— HOLIDAYS —

LO! the holiday season draws near
   And the question is: How shall we spend it?
Shall we patronize Margate, this year,
Where, I'm told, they've repainted the pier?
   Shall we visit Boulong?
   Or go south to Mong Blong
      And ascend it?
Shall we cross to The Hague – which is merely a
      step –
Or enjoy the sea-bathing at Dieppe?

Though the weather's too sultry, I feel,
   For a trip to Morocco or Venice,
Far away we might secretly steal
To a cottage at Dornoch or Deal,
   Or Le Touquet, methinks,
   Where they've excellent links
      And lawn tennis.

There's Skegness, too, "so bracing" (the posters
    report)
While Bexhill is a "winsome" resort!

But whatever our holidays are –
    If we sail a small dinghy at Dover,
If we tour through the Lakes in a car,
If we lounge at Ostend in a bar –
    In a fortnight, I know,
    We shall long for them so
        To be over!
It's delightful, of course, to make plans, and to
    pack,
But it's pleasanter far to get back!

THE
— NEIGHBOURS —

I ENVY not the rich who tread
Their marble stairs in Piccadilly;
Cocottages at Maidenhead
    Leave me completely chilly;
I do not need, and never shall,
A Palace on the Grand Canal.

No Stately Home, no grand Château,
    Described by Baedeker or Murray,
Would I exchange for "Mon Repos,"
    My little place in Surrey,
Which is indeed, in ev'ry sense,
A "Charming Bijou Residence."

Life runs in a familiar groove:
    The morning spent in giving orders
To John, the gard'ner, to remove
    The groundsel from the borders;
While in the afternoon I feed
The goldfish, or uproot a weed.

But when, at five o'clock, I try
    To gain some respite from my labours,
My peace too oft is broken by
    An influx of The Neighbours.
They ambush me on ev'ry side,
Before I have a chance to hide.

When, in my oldest clothes arrayed,
    I lounge at leisure in the garden,
Out comes Elaine (our parlourmaid)
    And says: "Oh sir, beg pardon!
But, please, the Rector's come to call;
I've left 'im in the outer 'all!"

And when at last that visit ends
    (The Vicar always stays for ages!),
Old Colonel Boreham brings some friends
    To see my saxifrages,
Or Mrs Wiggs from "Eversleigh"
Drops in to have a cup of tea.

One day, as I proposed to take
    A snooze – so grateful and reviving –
I saw Sir Corne and Lady Craik
    At my front door arriving,
So hid behind a large settee,
Before they could catch sight of me.

Elaine, alas! – a deadly sin
    For which she afterwards was chidden –
Without enquiry, showed them in
    To where their host was hidden;
And down they sat, two yards away,
While in an agony I lay!

I felt the meanest worm of worms,
    To crouch so close beside them, quailing,
While they discussed in candid terms
    My each and ev'ry failing;
Nor was the situation eased
When, quite by accident, I sneezed!

Who can describe what then befell?
    Its like was never drawn or painted!
For while the lady gave a yell,
    Threw up her hands and fainted,
Her spouse (who *never* sees a joke)
Was so upset he had a stroke!

Am I unsociable, ingrate?
    I must be; otherwise how is it
I fail so to appreciate
    The honour of a visit
From those who come for miles to call
On folks they do not know at all?

I feel more strongly ev'ry hour
    That though I need my income badly,
I would exchange it all for pow'r
    To suffer neighbours gladly;
Yes, I'd surrender all my pelf
To love The Neighbours as myself!

— PERSPECTIVE —

"It is sad and humiliating, but true, that our humanity is a matter of geography." – *Pall Mall Gazette*.

WHEN told that twenty thousand Japs
   Are drowned in a typhoon,
We feel a trifle shocked, perhaps,
   But neither faint nor swoon.
"Dear me! How tragic!" we repeat;
   "Ah, well! Such things must be!"
Our ordinary lunch we eat
   And make a hearty tea;
Such loss of life (with shame I write)
Creates no loss of appetite!

When on a Rocky Mountain ranch
   Two hundred souls, all told,
Are buried in an avalanche,
   The tidings leave us cold.
"Poor fellows!" we remark. "Poor things!
   All crushed to little bits!"
Then go to *Bunty Pulls the Strings*,
   Have supper at the Ritz,
And never even think again
Of land-slides in the State of Maine!

But when the paper we take in
    Describes how Mr Jones
Has slipped on a banana-skin
    And broken sev'ral bones,
"Good Heavens! What a world!" we shout;
    "Disasters never cease!
What *is* the Government about?
    And *where* are the Police?"
Distraught by such appalling news
All creature comforts we refuse!

Though plagues exterminate the Lapp,
    And famines ravage Spain,
They move us not like some mishap
    To a suburban train.
Each foreign tale of fire or flood,
    How trumpery it grows
Beside a broken collar-stud,
    A smut upon the nose!
For Charity (alas! how true!)
Begins At Home – and ends there, too!

THE HOMES OF
— LONDON —

After Mrs Hemans

THE happy homes of London,
   How beautiful they stand!
The crowded human rookeries
   That mar this Christian land.
Where cats in hordes upon the roof
   For nightly music meet,
And the horse, with non-adhesive hoof,
   Skates slowly down the street.

The merry homes of London!
   Around bare hearths at night,
With hungry looks and sickly mien,
   The children wail and fight.
There woman's voice is only heard
   In shrill, abusive key,
And men can hardly speak a word
   That is not blasphemy.

The healthy homes of London!
   With weekly wifely wage,
The hopeless husbands, out of work,
   Their daily thirst assuage.
The overcrowded tenement
   Is comfortless and bare,
The atmosphere is redolent
   Of hunger and despair.

The blessed homes of London!
   By thousands, on her stones,
The helpless, homeless, destitute,
   Do nightly rest their bones.

On pavements Piccadilly way,
   In slumber like the dead,
Their wan pathetic forms they lay,
   And make their humble bed.

The free, fair homes of London!
   From all the thinking throng,
Who mourn a nation's apathy,
   The cry goes up, "How long!"
And those who love old England's name,
   Her welfare and renown,
Can only contemplate with shame
   The homes of London town.

— NECESSITY —

LATE last night I slew my wife,
  Stretched her on the parquet flooring;
I was loth to take her life,
But I *had* to stop her snoring!

THE LAST HORSED
— 'BUS —

FARE thee well, thou plum-faced driver,
  Poised upon thine airy seat!
Final, ultimate survivor
  Of an order obsolete!
Fare thee well! Thy days are numbered.
Long, full long, by weight encumbered,
Tardily thy team hath lumbered
  Down each London street,
Passed by carts, bath-chairs, and hearses,
And the cause of constant curses!

Ancient Omnibus ungainly,
  We shall miss thee, day by day,
When thy swift successors vainly
  We with signals would delay;
When upon their platforms perching,
With each oscillation lurching,
We are perilously searching
  For the safest way
To alight without disaster,
While we speed each moment faster!

As our means of locomotion,
  Year by year, more deadly grow,
We shall think with fond devotion
  Of thy stately gait and slow.
Harassed, vexed, fatigued, and flurried
Shaken, discomposed, and worried,
As in motors we are hurried
  Wildly to and fro,
We perchance shall not disparage
Horse-drawn omnibus or carriage!

— LORD GORBALS —

ONCE, as old Lord Gorbals motored
Round his moors near John o' Groats,
He collided with a goatherd
And a herd of forty goats.
By the time his car got through
They were all defunct but two.

Roughly he addressed the goatherd:
"Dash my whiskers and my corns!
Can't you teach your goats, you dotard,
That they ought to sound their horns?
Look, my AA badge is bent!
I've a mind to raise your rent!"

THE MODEL
— MOTORIST —

Sir Thomas Lipton, when stopped by the Chertsey police for "scorching," remarked: "You have your duty to do, boys. I have always found you to be correct. I'm sorry."

YE murderous, motoring scorchers,
    With manners of Gadarene hogs,
Inflicting unspeakable tortures
    On children and chickens and dogs;
Alarming your fellows with hoots and with
      bellows,
    And filling their infants with terror,
Their cattle stampeding, and never conceding
    That *you* could perhaps be in error,
Who fall upon Fido and squash little Florrie,
And hasten away without saying you're sorry!

O listen, I beg, *con amore*,
    Pray pause in your Juggernaut flight,
And hark, while I tell you the story
    Of Lipton, that chivalrous knight!
When charged with exceeding the limit of
      speeding
    By constables ambushed in Chertsey,
He scorned to tell "whoppers" or browbeat those
      "coppers,"
    But, donning (with marvellous court'sy)
The smile that he wears at a ball or a "swarry,"
Remarked: "You are always correct, boys. I'm
      sorry!"

With awe and respect did each "cop" watch
    A creature so rare, so unique,
Who questioned no constable's stop-watch,
    Who showed neither temper nor pique,

But said, "Do your duty!" in tones rich and
    fruity,
    Admitting at once his transgression,
Content to take *their* word, with never a swear-
    word,
    To leave an unpleasant impression;
Exclaiming – his parents were Irish – "Begorry!
'Tis me that's the scorcher, and faith, bhoys, I'm
    sorry!"

Then follow his brilliant example,
    Ye chauffeurs to "joy-riding" prone,
And seek by apologies ample
    For sins of the past to atone.
Your pace do not quicken when dog or when
    chicken
    In "bonnet" or brake gets entangled,
Nor fly in a flutter, and leave in the gutter
    The man whom your motor has mangled;
But after you've pounced like a hawk on your
    quarry,
Just stop for a moment, and say that you're sorry!

— TABLE MANNERS —

ON the question of behaviour when At Table
There is much that proves perplexing to the
mind;
Should we eat, that is, as much as we are able?
    Should we drink as much as Nature feels
    inclined?
Is it right to use a spoon to swallow curry?
    Is it wrong to use a knife for eating cheese?
There is scope for much embarrassment and
    worry
        In such knotty points as these.

Of the business of eating and of drinking –
    Which are separate, distinctive,
    well-defined –
There is no one but must acquiesce in thinking
    That these functions should by no means be
    combined;
Since the man who fills his mouth with beef or
    pheasant,
        And proceeds to sluice it down with bitter beer,
Is a person whom at meals it isn't pleasant
        For his fellows to sit near.

Save for purposes of casual conversation,
　　You should always keep your mouth shut
　　　when you chew,
For the processes of oral mastication
　　Are not suitable for popular review;
And it shows a lack of manners or of breeding
　　To make noises like an infant with the croup,
Or adopt a loud and blatant mode of feeding,
　　　When ingurgitating soup.

Then, again, we do not need to be instructed
　　That our victuals must not ever be *inhaled*,
And that no one who is properly conducted
　　Will be guilty of the scandal thus entailed,
When a burst of unpremeditated laughter
　　Sends the glass of rare old port that you imbibe
Coursing lungwards – and the scene that follows
　　after
　　　'Twere not fitting to describe!

Let me tell you of my favourite Aunt Anna,
　　Who (though eighty) is alert and full of fun;
She inhaled the greater part of a banana,
　　When at luncheon once I chanced to make a
　　　pun.
All in vain the doctors probed and ordered
　　massage,
　　My relation is deprived of half a lung,
For the plantain in her pulmonary passage
　　　Is imbedded like a bung!

If you seek a second helping from the "slavey,"
    Should you leave the knife and fork upon your
        plate –
When the handles will be smeared with grease and
        gravy –
    Or retain them in your clutches while you
        wait?
O my Readers, pray be open to persuasion,
    And admit (what I have preached for many
        years)
That the knife and fork, on ev'ry such occasion,
        Should be placed *behind the ears*.

If asparagus or artichokes be handed,
    Do not view them with a terror-stricken eye,
Nor permit yourself a coward to be branded
    By allowing such a dish to pass you by.
Ev'ry stick (or leaf), when dipt in melted butter,
    Should be held between the finger-tips with
        grace,
And then flung, without a tremor or a flutter,
        Through the port-hole of your face.

Never scatter bits of food upon your clothing;
    Never harbour mashed potatoes in your beard;
You will find that people gaze at you with
        loathing,
    If some spinach to your eyebrow has adhered.
Last of all (I mean it kindly, Gentle Reader),
    If you cannot keep your fingers off a bone –
If, in fact, you are a gross or careless feeder –
        You had better feed alone!

— LUNCHEON —

To entertain one's friends at lunch –
Singly or in a solid bunch –
This is indeed a daily joy,
A pastime that can never cloy!

The restaurant that you select,
If you would win the world's respect,
Must be some centre of renown,
The most expensive place in town,
Where guests, in admiration lost,
Delight to think how much they cost,
And he is deemed the nicest host
Who manages to spend the most.

My brother Fritz, one summer's day,
Was lunching with his *fiancée*,
But must, I think, have lost his wits,
For when he got her to the Ritz
He ordered Irish stew for two
(A thing no gentleman would do),
And then, instead of quails or snipe,
A mayonnaise of tepid tripe,
And finished up this ghastly meal
With *vol-au-vent* of jellied eel!

You can imagine what ensued –
With what disgust poor Mabel viewed
The offal heaped upon her plate,
And how her love was turned to hate!

The lovelight faded from her eyes,
As sunshine pales in wintry skies;
The tears she was too proud to wipe
Went trickling down into the tripe;
The scorn that she could not conceal
Was mirrored in each jellied eel!
Passion lay dead; Romance took wing;
She gave her lover back his ring!

To-day, with Mabel at the Ritz
Some more fastidious lover sits,
While at some restaurant unknown,
Fritz eats pigs' trotters, all alone.

— WASTE —

I HAD written to Aunt Maud,
Who was on a trip abroad,
When I heard she'd died of cramp,
Just too late to save the stamp.

— DINNER —

DINNER was once a solemn meal;
Our fathers ate, straight off the reel,
Two soups, two fishes, entrées, roast,
A bird, sweets, savoury on toast,
Till from dessert at last they rose,
Well surfeited and comatose.

At such a feast we gaze askance,
To-day we only dine to dance.
The saxophone's melodious bleat,
The drummer's contrapuntal beat
Are mandates none may now ignore;
They bid us rise and take the floor!
But ere we spring from table, so,
To tread, on light fantastic toe,
Some measure frankly anthropoid,
We *must* make sure our mouths are void!

Young Henry Jones, a friend of mine,
Once took a girl to dance and dine;
And when she heard the saxophones
She turned at once to Henry Jones
And, laughing, dragged him to his feet.
His mouth was filled with *saumon-truite*
And also *pommes de terre au beurre*
(Or fish and chips, if you prefer),
And as they circled, cheek to cheek,
His mouth, alas! too full to speak,
He could not with becoming grace
Keep chewing in his partner's face,
So tried to swallow, at one gulp,
The scarcely masticated pulp!

Ah me! While he was acting thus,
Firmly in his œsophagus
A fish-bone (as his friends alleged)
Became inextricably wedged!

He choked! He ceased to breathe at all!
His partner then began to call
For doctors, and, I understand,
No less than four were close at hand,
If we include upon our list
A well-known osteologist.
(For in these dancing-clubs, you know,
The *monde* is very *comme il faut*;
An ex-Lord Chancellor was there,
Some ladies with peroxide hair,
A few *jeunes derniers* of the stage,
Two peeresses of riper age,
And others, not perhaps so *bien*
But having what the French call *chien*,
And wearing that décoll'té dress
Which makes one hope – but I digress!)

While four physicians scraped and bowed,
Each begging he might be allowed
To let his colleague take the case,
Poor Jones grew blacker in the face,
And seemed the symptoms to evince
Of some expiring Indian prince!

For hours the doctors argued hard
(The Bone-setter, of course, was barred)
Before they could at last agree
How best to split the patient's fee.
By then poor Henry Jones had tired
Of the discussion, and expired!

The moral, at a single glance,
Is this: If you *must* dine and dance,
Make sure the fish upon your plate
Is totally invertebrate;
If you decide to dance *and* dine,
See that your salmon has no spine!

THE MEN FROM
— BLANKLEY'S —

Owing to the dearth of dancing men, says the *Daily Mirror*,
hostesses are placed in a decided dilemma. The "entertain-
ment manager" of a well-known firm of universal providers
is, however, prepared to supply a score or so of dancing
guests at a few hours' notice.

AT Romford House the ball-room floor
  Mirrored a hostess somewhat flustered;
The débutantes around the door
   In mournful groups were clustered;
The band conversed in undertones,
   Their leader shrugged a scornful shoulder,
The draught about the chaperones
   Blew cold and ever colder;
The butler, on the stairs, grew pale,
He was, alas! the only male.

The rooms became as chill as vaults,
   Devoid of all but female dancers;
In vain the bandsmen played a waltz,
   A two-step and some Lancers.
The hostess, growing less alert,
   Secured an easy chair to nod on;
The maidens' waists remained ungirt,
   The matrons' toes untrod on;
Until the butler, with a groan,
Rushed headlong to the telephone.

The clock struck two as from the street
   There rose a sound, sublime, seraphic:
The steady tramp of manly feet
   Above the roar of traffic!
And Blankley's troupe of well-trained guests,

In clothes from Mr Clarkson rented,
   With "evening vests" whose low-cut chests
      Bore crimson 'kerchiefs, scented,
With carefully pomatum'd hair,
Ascended Lady Romford's stair!

Let poets tell how Roman geese
   Secured the Capitol from capture;
How Jason gained the Golden Fleece
   Let bards narrate with rapture.
Upon my tablets is engraved
   A deed more splendid still (and subtler),
Whereby the Romford ball was saved
   By Bellinger, the butler.
When Blankley nobly filled the breach
With guests at half a guinea each!

— PROVIDENCE —

FATE moves in a mysterious way,
As shown by Uncle Titus,
Who unexpectedly, one day,
Was stricken with St Vitus.
It proved a blessing in disguise,
For, thanks to his condition,
He won the Non-Stop Dancing Prize
At Wembley Exhibition.

— DANCING —

WHEN the parquet has been polished, and
all furniture abolished,
And the band has made a serviceable start;
When your programme is selected, and your
efforts are directed
To indulgence in the Saltatory Art;
When your fellow-dancers eye you, as they sail
serenely by you
With a scornful supercilious sort of glance,
There is nothing half so rotten as to find you have
forgotten
How to dance.

There are many kinds of dances, from that
favourite of France's
Which some people call a "valse" and others
"waltz" –
(Though the French, in doubtful taste, dance both
the *can-can* and the *waist*-dance,
These are vulgar, and have many other faults) –
To the saraband of Prussia, and the rigadoon of
Russia,
Which demand the greatest energy and zeal –
From that not-to-be-ignored dance which the
Scottish term a "Sword-dance,"
To a reel.

When your grandmamma went dancing, her
behaviour was entrancing;
Such decorum, so much grace, were rarely
seen!
And her too impatient lover was compelled, alas!
to hover

On the outskirts of her spacious crinoline.
While demurely minuetting in a staid and sober
 setting,
 She religiously maintained her self-respect;
When she plied the "light fantastic," every pose,
 however plastic,
  Was *correct*.

What a pleasing variation from the present
 generation
 To whom dancing is a mere athletic sport,
Which if people toil a lot at they can get extremely
 hot at –
 Just a form of taking exercise, in short!
Men, inspired by flute and fiddle, grasp their
 partners round the middle,
 And revolve till they can scarcely stand
  upright,
While their cousins and their sisters dance their
 little feet to blisters,
  Ev'ry night.

Moral

Now the moral of my story, which I dwell on *con amore*,
    Is that dancing is no mere gymnastic game;
While for anyone desiring either romping or perspiring
    There are numerous pursuits that I could name.
And the youth who yells and hollers and is forced to change his collars
    Should not ever be permitted to take part
In the dance which (for the *last* time, let me say) is *not* a pastime,
        But an Art.

THE BATTUE OF — BERLIN —

A Long Way After Southey

During the Tsar's visit to Berlin last year the German Emperor entertained his Royal suite at a battue, at which, "in favourable weather," says the *Daily Mail*, "492 stags were killed during an hour's shooting."

IT was a winter's morning,
  The Kaiser's sport was done;
From far and near the driven deer
  Had faced the Royal "gun,"*
And all around, in grim array,
Five hundred rotting corpses lay.

*"Rifle" does not rhyme.

From near and far, to King and Tsar
   The startled herds had fled;
And many a stag had swelled the bag,
   And many a hind lay dead.
Such things must be and will in short,
After a famous hour of sport!

It was the German Emperor
   Who slew five hundred deer;
But what he killed so many for
   Is not completely clear.
But all the journalists report
That 'twas a famous morning's sport.

From left and right, in furious flight,
   The stags to slaughter came;
Each beast, deceased, by death increased
   This holocaust of game.
And, after all (you may retort),
It was a famous morning's sport.

Let sportsmen raise their hymns of praise
   To those who made such bags,
Who in an hour evinced the pow'r
   To slay five hundred stags,
While I repeat (how dare you snort?)
That 'twas a famous morning's sport!

THE ENGLISHMAN'S
— HOME —

I WAS playing golf the day
That the Germans landed;
All our troops had run away,
All our ships were stranded;
And the thought of England's shame
Altogether spoilt my game.

— THE SPORTSMAN —

THE lover, in Edwardian times,
     Whose heart had taken sev'ral tosses
Would rush to Equatorial climes
     To shoot rhinoceroses;
His soul found solace in the cry
Of stricken hippopotami.

The swain whose lady proved unkind
     Would fly from her capricious humours,
And creature comfort seek to find
     In extirpating pumas;
His sense of misery he'd lose
When he had killed some kangaroos.

Alas! Our English youth to-day
     Who never falls a slave to passion –
And, if he did, would not allay
     His grief in such a fashion –
Unlike his am'rous forbears, lacks
The stimulus to slaughter yaks.

*

My Uncle Claud, in early life,
     Adored Aunt Mabel blindly, madly.
Though, later, she became his wife,
     She used him then so badly
That there was nothing he could do
But go and hunt for caribou.

Although she threatened to relent,
     He brushed aside her lame excuses
And off to Canada he went,

In search of moose (or mooses),
To scour each prairie and plateau
For bison and for buffalo.

Now, in his house in Eaton Square,
    Where he resides with dear Aunt Mabel,
The sporting trophies ev'rywhere,
    On floor and wall and table,
Recall the days of long ago
When she persistently said: "No!"

A splendid stuffed orang-outang
    Within the dining-room is standing,
While herds of guilty chamois hang
    Their heads on ev'ry landing,
And floors are strewn with crocodiles
That greet your feet with frozen smiles.

But though his skill with rod and gun
    Congests my uncle's house with trophies,
He has, alas! an only son
    Who such a perfect oaf is,
He takes no interest in sport,
Except the purely English sort.

A first-class shot, he loves to stride
    Through turnips with his old retriever;
Most gallantly to hounds he'll ride
    When hunting with the Belvoir;
His language, too, is of a kind
That leaves the Master's far behind!

And yet he seems much more inclined
    Idly with dog and gun to potter
Than to pursue the carted hind
    Or spear the drowning otter;
He somehow doesn't care a scrap
For shooting pigeons from a trap.

When hounds have run a fox to earth,
    And some one digs it out and brains it,
He feels no tendency to mirth,
    Or, if he does, restrains it;
And when he sees a rabbit coursed
His laughter is distinctly forced.

Though he was crossed in love, last fall,
    And jilted by Lord Oxhed's daughter,
He did not hear the Tropics call,
    Or feel the lust of slaughter;
He did not hasten East to shoot
A wombat or a bandicoot.

Compelled to sacrifice all hope
    Of winning back his faithless charmer,
He never stalked an antelope,
    A mountain-goat or llama;
Unlike his father, Uncle Claud,
He never even went abroad!

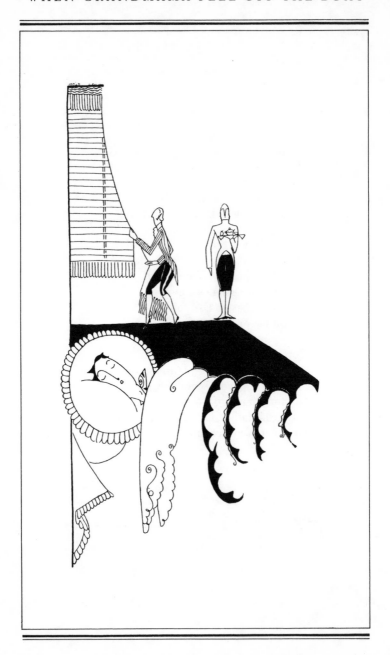

— GETTING UP —

THOUGH many men have made their mark
By rising daily with the lark,
'Tis not a plan I recommend;
The practice no one can defend.

For Man to emulate the beast
Is quite absurd, to say the least,
But if you *must*, then try to find
A bird of some more torpid kind,
Content in slumber to recline
Till half-past eight or even nine.

Then let a stealthy menial creep
Within the chamber where you sleep,
In silence draw the blind half up
And at your elbow place a cup
Of tea, with buttered bread to suit,
Or, if you should prefer it, fruit.

But if the latter food you choose,
Take care what kind of fruit you use!
I recollect, in early life,
I loved our local surgeon's wife.
I ate an apple ev'ry day,
To keep the doctor far away!

Alas! he was a jealous man
And grew suspicious of my plan.
He'd noticed sev'ral pips about
When taking my appendix out
(A circumstance that must arouse
Suspicions in the blindest spouse),
And, though I squared the thing somehow,
I always eat bananas now!

— THE IDEAL HUSBAND —

A recent correspondence in the *Daily Mirror* proves that, according to popular opinion, fools make the best husbands. "The bigger the fool," as one writer briefly puts it, "the better the husband."

THOUGH husbands bright and brainy
  May have their use, one knows,
Give me an honest zany
  As partner of my woes!
How blest indeed is woman's fate
Who takes a noodle as her mate!

The clever husband quarrels,
  Or grumbles at his food;
The wit's ideas of morals
  Are lamentably crude;
A partner with a feeble mind
Is neither vicious nor unkind.

'Tis commonly admitted,
  And ev'ry one allows,
That if a man's half-witted
  He makes a perfect spouse;
And more resigned, each day, I feel
To marriage with an imbecile!

When comes my time for mating,
  When Cupid shoots his bolt,
I don't mind frankly stating
  That I shall wed a dolt.
He must be dull who marries me;
But (as you say) he's bound to be!

— LOVE'S HANDICAP —

FROM the earliest days,
  Ev'ry writer of lays
    Has delighted to sing about Passion;
But of rhymes there's a dearth
For the Briton by birth
    Who would follow this popular fashion.
For though Love is a theme
That we poets esteem
    As unrivalled, immortal, sublime too,
'Tis a word that the bard
Finds it daily more hard
    To discover a suitable rhyme to!
For one can't always mention the "stars up
      above,"
    Ev'ry time that one talks about Love!

When the French *troubadour*
Wants to sing of *l'amour*
    No such lyrical fetters restrain him;
And when making *la cour*
To his mistress, *chaqu' jour*,
    There's no famine of rhyme to detain him.
He'll describe, *sans détours*,
How as soft as *velours*
    Is her hand, and her voice like a fiddle;
How they ate *petits fours*
Till she cried: "*Au secours!*"
    When his arm went *autour* of her middle!
And there's no need for *him* to refer to her
      "glove,"
    Just because he's discoursing on Love!

The Venetian *signor*
Who discusses *l'amor'*
   To his lady-love's balcony climbing,
As he presses her *fior'*
To his bosom (*al' cuor'*)
   Has no trouble at all about rhyming!
When with frenzied *furor'*
And such fervent *calor'*
   He suggests her becoming his *sposa*,
What for him does the trick
Is that rhymes are as thick
   As the leaves upon fair Vallombrosa;
And he never need liken his dear to a "dove,"
   Ev'ry time that he sings about Love!

'Tis the absence of rhymes
That inclines me, at times,
   To renounce any mention of Cupid,
And, instead, to write odes
To (say) skylarks or toads,
   Though it may seem faint-hearted or stupid.
For it's easy to sing
Of the sunshine or Spring,
   And of Pan (or some mythical person),
But to find a fresh rhyme
For the Passion sublime
   That we bards are supposed to write verse on –
Well, I'm tempted to give the whole question "the
     shove"
   And to sing no more songs about Love!

MRS CHRISTOPHER
— COLUMBUS —

THE bride grows pale beneath her veil,
  The matron, for the nonce, is dumb,
Who listens to the tragic tale
  Of Mrs Christopher Columb;
Who lived and died (so says report)
A widow of the herbal sort.

Her husband upon canvas wings
  Would brave the ocean, tempest-tost,
He had a *culte* for finding things
  Which nobody had ever lost,
And Mrs C. grew almost frantic
When he discovered the Atlantic.

But nothing she could do or say
  Would keep her Christopher at home.
Without delay he sailed away,
  Across what poets call "the foam,"
While neighbours murmured, "What a shame!"
(And wished their husbands did the same.)

But Mrs C. remained indoors,
  And poked the fire and wound the clocks,
Amused the children, scrubbed the floors,
  Or darned her absent husband's socks.
(For she was far too sweet and wise
To darn the great explorer's eyes.)

And when she chanced to look around
   At all the couples she had known,
She realised how few had found
   A home as peaceful as her own,
And saw how pleasant it may be
To wed a chronic absentee.

Her husband's absence she enjoyed,
   Nor ever asked him where he went,
Thinking him harmlessly employed
   Discovering some continent.
Had he been always in, no doubt,
Some day she would have found him out.

A melancholy thing it is
   How few have known or understood
The manifold advantages
   Of such herbaceous widowhood!
What is it ruins married lives
But husbands? (Not to mention wives?)

O wedded couples of to-day,
   Pray take these principles to heart,
And copy the Columbian way
   Of living happily apart,
And so, to *you*, at any rate,
Shall marriage be a "blessed state."

THE TRUCKS OF
— TRURO —

A Ballad for the Boudoir

A writer in *Punch* declares that the saddest sight he ever saw
was a row of dispirited trucks standing in a siding, on each of
which was painted the bitter words, "This truck not to go
East of Truro."

WHEN the waters of the Douro
 Flow up-country from the sea;
When these trucks go East of Truro,
 Then my heart will faithless be!
Sparkling like some rich liqueur, oh!
Tender, delicate and pure, oh!
As Bellini's *chiaroscuro*,
 Is the love that kindles me!
When these trucks go East of Truro,
 Then will I be false to thee!

Though the clerk forget his bureau,
 I will not forgetful be!
Though these trucks go East of Truro,
 Thou shalt not go East of me!
Though each celebrated Euro-
Pean oculist or neuro-
Path, when he effects a cure, o-
 Mit to take his patient's fee!
Though these trucks go East of Truro,
 I will still have truck with thee!

— THE NEW ROMANCE —

"A romantic story attaches to the engagement of Mr D——
M—— and Miss N—— S——, which was the outcome of
the former's prowess in the international polo matches." –
Central News.

WHEN first she fell in love with Frank,
　'Twas not the latter's youth and rank,
Nor yet his balance at the bank
　　That won the heart of Elsie;
'Twas not the whiteness of his soul
That made her lose all self-control,
But 'twas the way he kicked a goal,
　　When playing "back" for Chelsea.
'Twas this inspired the girl's affection,
And turned her thoughts in Frank's direction.

But when, at Lord's, with bitter sobs,
She saw her sweetheart score two blobs,
Defeated by the googly lobs
　　Of Patrick Brown (of Dover);
And Brown, to further efforts spurred,
Took one more wicket, and a third,
Her love she speedily transferred
　　(He'd bowled the maiden over!);
When, as I say, he did the "hat-trick,"
She promptly fell in love with Patrick!

This flame, alas! was doomed to die.
As she was golfing, last July,
The Rev'rend Mr Jones passed by
　　(That well-known sporting cleric).
He drove superbly from the tee;
Said Elsie: "That's the man for me!"
And when he did a hole in three
　　(The seventh at North Berwick),

As from the green she watched him strutting,
She loved the parson for his putting!

Yet, when at Wimbledon she met
A man named Smith, who, in *one* set,
Served forty faults into the net,
   In the most futile fashion,
Instead of feeling shocked or chilled
At sight of service so unskilled,
The maiden's heart with pity filled,
   And pity led to passion!

✳

They spent the honeymoon in Venice,
Where, luckily, there's no lawn-tennis!

— GOOD SPORT —

"Business," says Mr Selfridge, "is the best of all sports."

SOME sportsmen love to stalk the stag,
To trawl for tarpon or for tunny,
To course the hare, to run a "drag,"
Or (with some ferrets in a bag)
    Evict the harmless bunny;
To thread a minnow on a hook
And fish in some familiar brook.

Commercial sports I much prefer;
    To stalk a public shallow-pated,
To angle for each customer
And capture him (or, rather, her)
    On hooks with "bargains" baited;
The willing client to ensnare,
And lure the shy one from his lair!

Some sportsmen love to hear the sound
    Of partridge calling in the clover,
The huntsman's horn, the yelp of hound
(Denoting that a fox is found),
    The cry of "Woodcock over!"
The distant "honk" of homing goose,
The savage roar of mating moose!

All these are sweet, I'm bound to say,
    But give me sounds more picturesque, please,
As: "Madam, kindly step this way!"
"What can we show you, Miss, to-day?"
    Or, "Pay it at the desk, please!"
To tastes as mercantile as mine
No cry is half so sweet as "Sign!"

— THE BUSY RICH —

"It is impossible for a rich man to be idle," says Lord Kesteven. "The richer he is the harder he works."

WHEN I had a hundred a year,
　　I led a most leisurely life;
All work I would shun, as I sat in the sun,
　　Where I whittled a stick with a knife.
In youth I was lazy and idle, I fear,
When I had a hundred, a hundred a year!

When I had five hundred a year,
　　My labours appeared to augment;
I rose with the lark, and would dress in the dark,
　　And by Tube to the City I went.
From eight to six-thirty I worked as cashier,
When I had five hundred, five hundred a year!

When I had a thousand a year,
　　More diligent daily I grew;
I would breakfast at nine (if the weather was fine),
　　And I stayed at the office till two.
The brainwork was heavy, the strain was severe,
When I had a thousand, a thousand a year!

When I had ten thousand a year,
　　No respite from toil I enjoyed;
I went to dull balls, and paid afternoon calls,
　　And shot grouse (for the poor Unemployed).
I hired an estate, with a park full of deer,
When I had ten thousand, ten thousand a year!

With seventy thousand a year,
　　My work ev'ry moment grows more;
I buy motor-cars, and I open bazaars,
　　And I struggle to fill up Form IV.
And oft I recall, with a sigh or a tear,
My leisurely life on a hundred a year!

— THE MORNING —

HOW slowly do the mornings pass
For members of that leisured class
Whose ancestors, by striking oil,
Have saved them from a life of toil!
Those dreary hours from 10 to 1 –
Nothing accomplished, nothing done –
Increase the mental *ennui* which
Is such a bugbear to the rich!

And yet, though thoughts of boredom irk
And drive some men to honest work,
Pause ere you take a step so rash,
For if you do not need the cash,
Mere labour for its own sweet sake
Is, you'll admit, a great mistake.

A millionaire who once I knew
Would slave away, the whole day through;
Leaving his couch at 8 a.m.
(A practice I for one condemn),

He'd leap into his car at nine
And, ev'ry morning, rain or shine,
Down to his City office hum,

Chewing a wad of scented gum
And reading the "Financial News"
(A paper I should never choose).

Once having reached his office chair,
This poor misguided millionaire
Would park his gum beneath his desk
(A habit none too picturesque)
And start in working right away,
Nor ever quit till close of day!

What happened? His neglected wife,
Compelled to lead a double life,
Eloped for sev'ral long week-ends
With one or other of his friends!
And while the neighbours said: "Tut-tut!
How she does fool that poor old Mutt!"
Oblivious of his wife's affairs,
He thought of naught but Bulls and Bears!

His daughters, too, from morn till night,
Freed from paternal oversight,
Went "movie-mad" and, if you please,
Absconded to Los Angeles!
And while they often might be seen
Featured as "stars" upon the screen,
Marrying actors of repute,
Divorcing those that didn't suit –
Fresh husbands each returning day
Hover around them as they play –
Heedless of what they might become,
Their father toiled and chewed his gum!

Meanwhile his son, quite uncontrolled –
A gump, but with a heart of gold –
Had forged his father's name on cheques
For members of the fairer sex,
And would have gone to jail, I know,
Had he not been too rich to go!

Immersed in business all day long,
My poor old friend thought nothing wrong,
And died, as happy as could be,
From overwork, at ninety-three.
Whereas, I venture to suggest,
If he had been content to rest
He might (had he remained alive)
Have lived to—— well, say, ninety-five!

— SLUSH —

Describing the scene at a railway station when schoolboys return home for the holidays, the *Daily Mail* says: "One small boy there was who had no mother to meet him. He stood, a lonely figure, till a big chauffeur came up and touched his cap.... He would rather have had a mother than a motor to meet him. You could read that in his pathetic little eyes."

DOWERED with the wealth of Ophir,
   Reared on costly caviare,
Driven by a foreign chauffeur
   In a spacious Siddeley car,
Luckless little Thompson minor
   Would have paid a handsome cheque
For a mother to entwine her
   Loving arms about his neck!
Though the motor's speed is greater,
Thompson much prefers "the mater!"

Long ago, with eyes all shiny,
   She had asked, in tender tone:
"Would you like a little tiny
   Baby-sister of your own?"
Now it stung him like a blister
   That he'd answered: "I should like,
Not a tiny baby-sister,
   But a full-sized motor-bike!"
That was why no fair relation
Welcomed Thompson at the station!

Other fellows had a mother;
    Sisters met them at the train.
As he watched them kiss each other,
    Thompson's heart was racked with pain.
Not a single fond, devoted
    Female waited for him there,
And with bitterness he quoted:
    "Can a motor's tender care . . . ?"
(This, you must admit, was crim'nal;
Boys should never quote the Hymnal.)

See, his friends, in cabs and taxis,
    Hold maternal fingers tight,
While poor Thomson minor waxes
    Sad and sadder at the sight!
For although, perhaps, he'd rather,
    At the hour of his return,
Have a motor than a father
    (Fathers can be harsh and stern!);
Can he hope his sobs to smother,
With a motor for a mother?

— WINTER SPORTS —

THE ice upon our pond's so thin
That poor Mama has fallen in!
We cannot reach her from the shore
Until the surface freezes more.
Ah me, my heart grows weary waiting –
Besides, I want to have some skating.

— L'ENFANT GLACÉ —

WHEN Baby's cries grew hard to bear
I popped him in the Frigidaire.
I never would have done so if
I'd known that he'd be frozen stiff.
My wife said: "George, I'm so unhappé!
Our darling's now completely *frappé*!"

— GRANDMAMA —

WHEN Grandmama was seventeen
And Queen Victoria was queen,
She wore a gown of bombazine
    And was a famous beauty;
She married Grandpapa (although
She much preferred another beau
Who played upon the piccolo)
    Because it was her duty
And not, you may be sure, becos
She knew how very rich he was.

They spent a perfect honeymoon
At Como in the month of June;
While Grandpa played on his bassoon
    Some airs that he'd invented,

She listened with her cheeks aglow,
And shortly (in a day or so)
Forgot her jilted piccolo
    And grew at last contented.
The happy pair were blessed by Fate:
They had a family of eight.

More fair each day dear Grandma grew;
Her eyes were of the palest blue,
Her ringlets of a raven hue
   (Or so her portraits tell us);
When as a bride she went about
She was the toast at drum or rout –
Grandpa, who suffered from the gout,
   Became extremely jealous,
Trying to tune up his bassoon
At moments most inopportune.

When Grandmama was thirty-three
Her life was peaceful as could be;
With children clustered round her knee
   She'd sit and do her knitting.
She wore a black lace cap and shawl,
And hardly ever moved at all,
Though sometimes she would pay a call
   (Weather, of course, permitting)
In mantle ruched with sarsenet
And bonnet trimmed with beads and jet.

Though gone the radiant bloom of youth,
As yet she'd hardly lost a tooth;
She was of riper years, in truth,
   But still her charms attracted.
Complexioned like an autumn rose
(Her portraits of that date disclose
The glossy and unpowdered nose
   That Fashion then exacted),
So elegant, though amply curved,
And wonderfully well preserved.

When Grandmama was fifty-five
She suddenly became alive,
Attended ev'ry Ping-Pong Drive
   And on her bike would pedal
To play a round at Forest Row
Where, taking half a stroke or so,
She very often beat the Pro.
   And gained the Monthly Medal.
At Cowes she won, by half a lap,
The Roller-skating Handicap.

She occupied a service-flat,
She wore a saucy Trilby hat,
A tailor-made and neat cravat,
   Was always in a hurry,
With energy that knew no bounds
She kept a pack of Basset hounds

And exercised them in the grounds
   Of Grandpa's seat in Surrey.

Her raven locks were tinged with grey,
But she grew younger ev'ry day.

When Grandmama was sixty-nine
She had acquired a taste for wine,
Wherever she was asked to dine
    She criticised the claret;

Her stories were a trifle strange
(She got them from the Stock Exchange),
On ev'ry subject she would range
    And chattered like a parrot.
At Bridge so stridently she joked
That her opponents all revoked.

When Grandmama was eighty-two
Her hair resumed its earlier hue
But with a touch of Navy blue
    And copper intermingled;
In vain her great-grandchildren raved
And said it made her look depraved,
She had it permanently waved
    And, naturally, shingled,

And Lasky (or some Movie-man)
Begged her to star in "Peter Pan."

She changed her style and taste in dress,
She paid much more and wore much less,
Till there was nothing left to guess
    Of what was veiled so slightly
By little frocks of crêpe Georgette
Which she would buy from Lafayette,
And, as she smoked her cigarette
    And quaffed her cocktails nightly,
The leaders of the new régime
Said Grandma was a perfect scream!

To-day, although she's ninety-four
At night-clubs still she takes the floor
With dancing partners by the score –
    You needn't deem them heroes,
For on the parquet she's so light,
And just the perfect weight and height.
I'm taking her myself to-night
    To sup and dance at Ciro's!
It's fun, of course – but, I foresee,
We shan't get home till after three!

THE MARTYRDOM OF
— FASHION —

The Dirge of the Directoire Dress, by Mlle Belle-Eel.

WHEN Worth and Paquin plan and plot
Designs and fashion-plates fantastic,
Heedless of those whose forms are not
Particularly plastic,
They little know what pain they cause
By disregarding Nature's laws.

Huge hats upon my head repose,
A whalebone collar cramps my throttle,
My patient shoulders slope, like those
Of any Perrier bottle;
And now, to please Parisian taste,
I've got to sacrifice my waist!

To suit a tailor's idle whim,
My helpless frame is shaped and moulded;
With silken fetters every limb
Is hobbled and enfolded.
O Worth, O Paquin, must my hips
Endure a permanent eclipse?

I cannot walk, I cannot sit;
My figure, altered and amended,
Is not, to say the least of it,
As Providence intended.
Ah, who can view without compassion
This modern Martyrdom of Fashion?

— DRESSING —

SOME people take an hour to dress;
It can be done in rather less
If you've a valet standing by
To lace your boots, and tie your tie,

To take your braces in a reef,
Put scent upon your handkerchief,
And, when the collar-stud you clasp
Falls from its owner's nerveless grasp
And rolls beneath the wash-hand-stand,
To place a second in your hand!

But if, alas! you chance to be
A member of the *bourgeoisie*
Whose sole indoor domestic aid
Consists of (say) a parlour-maid,
You cannot, like the *haute noblesse*,
Have someone present while you dress.

Yet you can choose your clothes with care:
For instance, 'twould be wrong to wear
A black tail-coat with yellow boots,

White waistcoats with your golfing suits

Or (specially if you're rotund)
Check knickers and a cummerbund!

A sweet disorder in the dress
May suit some poets, I confess,
But personally I admire
A certain neatness of attire;
I hold the very strongest views
About elastic-sided shoes,
While made-up ties and "dickeys" too
Are both of them, of course, taboo!
And collars made of celluloid
Are things you simply *must* avoid!

An absent-minded friend of mine,
Invited out, one night, to dine
At Oxford with a well-known Don,
Forgot to put his trousers on,
And out into the street he strode,
Oblivious of that moral code
Which lays it down as not genteel
To walk abroad *en deshabille*!

He was arraigned by the police,
And charged with Breeches of the Peace,
A crime he had to expiate
In trousers furnished by the State.

PLAGUES AT THE
— PLAY —

"Last night even the postprandial conversation of some well-dressed members of the audience failed to neutralise the effect of the music, though they did their best." – *The Times*.

"WELL-DRESSED," and well-fed, and
  well-meaning (God knows!),
 They arrive when the play is half ended;
As they pass to their stalls, through the tightly-
  packed rows,
They beruffle your hair and they tread on your
  toes,
 Quite unconscious of having offended!
Then they argue a bit as to how they shall sit,
 And uncloak in a leisurely fashion,
While they act as a blind to the people behind
 Who grow perfectly purple with passion;
Till at last, by the time they are seated and settled,
Their neighbours all round them are thoroughly
  nettled!

A programme, of course, they've forgotten to
    buy
    (This in audible accents they mention),
And whenever some distant attendant they spy,
They halloo or give vent to remarks such as "Hi!"
    In attempts to attract her attention.
After this (which is worse) they will loudly
    converse,
    And enjoy a good gossip together
On the clothes they have bought and the colds
    they have caught,
    On the state of the crops and the weather,
Till they leave, in the midst of some tense
    "situation,"
That's spoilt by their flow of inane conversation.

O managers, pray, am I asking too much
    If I beg that these "persons of leisure"
Be kept in a sound-proof and separate hutch,
If their nightly theatrical manners are such
    As to spoil other playgoers' pleasure?
For it can't be denied that a playhouse supplied
    With a cage for such talkative parrots,
Or a series of stalls (of the kind that have walls
    And some hay and a couple of carrots)
Would bestow on the public a boon and a blessing
And deal with an evil in need of redressing!

— CREATURE COMFORTS —

"What greater pleasure can there be to a private gentleman,"
says Karl Hagenbeck, in his *Beasts and Men*, "than that of
maintaining and establishing personal friendships with a
collection of foreign animals?"

FOR years I led a dreary life!
   The days passed slowly, one by one;
I fed the ducks, reproved my wife,
Played Handel's *Largo* on the fife,
    Or gave the dog a run.
I neither realised nor knew
The pleasures of a private Zoo.

I never loved a dear gazelle,
   To glad me with its soft black eye,
Nor ever to my lot it fell
To know a penguin really well,
    Till, early last July,
I bought a small menagerie,
And oh! the difference to me!

Now, when my spouse, perverse or cold,
   Induces an attack of dumps,
I feel encouraged and consoled
When in their *manège* I behold
    My camels' greater humps;
I fly from dear mama-in-law
To Kate, my talkative macaw.

When statesmen's speeches are disgraced
  By vulgar insults which denote
A lamentable lack of taste,
I seek my monkey-house in haste
    To find an antidote;
I turn for manners to the lair
Of Bosco, my performing bear.

Those "lions" whom we *fête* and feed,
  Heroes of sword or brush or pen,
Are they more dignified, indeed,
Than creatures of that nobler breed
    Which decorate my den?
The more my fellow-men I view,
The more I love my private Zoo!

— THE CHOICE —

A well-known lady dog-fancier informed a representative of the *Daily Mirror* that, in case of fire, she would most certainly save her dog rather than her husband.

"GO! Sound the fire alarm!" she cried.
"My house is all ablaze inside!
The flames are spreading far and wide;
 The air with smoke is laden!
My darling's in an upper room!
Oh, save him from a fiery tomb!"
Straight, as she spoke, through sparks and fume
 Came brave Lieutenant Sladen.
Quoth he: "The horsed-escape is here, ma'am;
We'll save your husband, never fear, ma'am!"

"My *husband*?" she replied. "Nay, nay!
Don't waste your time on *him*, I pray,
But turn your thoughts without delay
 To things that really matter.
For though my weaker-half's asleep,
A faithful lap-dog, too, I keep,
And if I hold the former cheap,
 I idolise the latter.
Gladly, to save the best of bow-wows,
I'd sacrifice," she sobbed, "my spou-ouse!

How prettily my nose he licks!
(I'm speaking of the dog) and pricks
His ears and barks, while as for tricks
　　He never seems to tire, man!
He'll balance sugar on his snout——"
From burning windows came a shout;
Her husband suddenly leaned out
　　And thus addressed the fireman:
"You've seen the sort of wife I cherish;
Then be humane and – let me perish!"

— A PLEA FOR PONTO —

Sir Frederick Banbury moved in the House of Commons:—
"That in the opinion of this House no operation for the
purpose of vivisection should be performed upon dogs."

WHEN you're studying the habits
　　Of the germ of German measles,
When you're searching out a cure for indigestion,
　　You may practise upon rabbits,
　　Upon guinea-pigs, or weasels,
If you think that they throw light upon the
　　　　question;
　　You may note how bad the bite is
　　Of the microbe of bronchitis,
By performing operations upon frogs,
　　But I've yet to hear the mention
　　Of a surgical invention
That can justify experiments on DOGS.

I would sooner people perished
  Of lumbago or swine-fever
(Or, at any rate, I'd rather they should chance it!)
  Than that any hound I cherished
  From a "pom" to a retriever,
Should be subject to the vivisector's lancet.
  I know nought of theoretics,
  But in spite of anæsthetics –
Ether, chloroform or other soothing drug –
  (Though perhaps I argue wrongly)
  I should disapprove most strongly,
If I found a person puncturing my pug!

  If we wish to make a bee-line
  For the chicken-pox bacillus,
From the hen-house there is nothing to debar us;
  We may learn from creatures feline
  What the causes are that kill us
When we suffer from infirmities *cat*arrhous!
  But when dogs' insides we study,
  Then our hands and hearts grow bloody,
And we needn't be a crank or partisan
  To display a strong objection
  To the so-called vivisection
Of that animal we style the Friend of Man!

THE DESERTED
— GARDEN —

THERE is a garden in our square,
And householders can have the key,
On payment of an annual fee;
Yet no one enters there!

From August till the first of May,
    This garden is an empty place;
    No puppy-dogs their tails may chase,
        No children romp and play!

Here faithful pug or Pekinese
    With chain and collar must be led,
    Lest he disturb some flower-bed
        That no one ever sees!

Here ragged urchins from the street
    Peer through the bars with wistful eyes
    On a deserted Paradise,
        Untrod by children's feet!

Some day, I know, with guilty grin,
    That garden gate I shall unlock,
    Collect this squalid little flock
        And lead them gaily in!

And, 'spite of by-laws and decrees,
    Poor Ponto's collar I'll detach,
    And let him run about and scratch,
        And scamper at his ease!

What matter then that neighbours glare
    At happy dog or grubby boys,
    If somebody at last enjoys
        The garden in our square?

— THE FALLEN STAR —

WHEN Ada Stew was seventeen
  No shyer girl was ever seen;
Her diffidence, her bashful mien,
  Astonished each beholder.
As waitress at a Corner-House,
Demure and timid as a mouse,
She served the drumstick of a grouse,
  The mutton's leg or shoulder,
With such an air of coy reserve
The gayest patrons lost their nerve.

Her skin was white as driven snow,
Yet, when she blushed, her cheeks would grow
Incarnadined, her gills would glow
  As rosy as the mullet.
If spoken to a trifle sharp,
Her mouth she'd open like a carp,
While sounds as of some Hebrew harp
  Would issue from her gullet,
Till customers exclaimed: "Poor fish!"
And left a tip beneath the dish.

Into that Corner-House, one day,
Two strangers from the USA
Were led by Providence to stray,
  In search of food and solace.
Their tempers were distinctly sour,
For they had wasted half an hour
Viewing The Abbey and The Tow'r,
  The Mint, The Tate, The Wallace,
And, wearied out, they wandered in
And called for clams and terrapin.

The latter was, alas! a word
That Ada Stew had never heard;
She wondered, was it beast or bird
    For which they were applying?
But with a recollection dim
Of reading in some psalm or hymn
Of terrapin and seraphim
    Continually crying,
She dropped her tray of Lager beers
And burst into a flood of tears.

Said Gus P. Sckunk: "This burg is bum!
Its food is punk, its dames are dumb!"*
"I'll tell the world!" said Al K. Sckum,
    His fellow film producer;
Then, to the Nippy at his side
Whose tears were flowing like the tide,
"Say, baby, what's your name?" he cried.
    She answered: "Ada Stew, sir!"

*Do American film directors talk like this? – *Pub*.
  Poetic licence. – *H.G.*

She wept as though her heart would break.
The Corner-House became a lake.

Al looked at Gus, and Gus at Al.
"We've searched the earth to find a gal
Sufficiently ee-mo-tion-*al*
    To suit our noo production,
And see what Fate hands out to us!
I guess this pop-eyed Jane," said Gus,
"Has got a goldarned ge-ni-us
    For lachrymal effluxion!"
"I'll tell the world!" said Al K. Sckum,
Then turned to Ada and said: "Come!"

They whisked her off to Hollywood
Where, as may well be understood,
Her sobstuff qualities made good
    And as a "star" she glittered.
The tears she spouted like a tap
Washed all her rivals off the map,
And movie-fans were forced to clap
    (While only groundlings tittered)
When Ada Stew was billed, one day,
As "Adelina Fricassée."

Then "Talkies" took the world by storm;
No longer would the public swarm
To gaze at simple grace of form
    Or mere expressive features.
But when poor Adelina spoke,
Her voice the harshest echoes woke,
She seemed (if you'll excuse a joke)
    The meanest of God's screechers!
She cracked the discs of gramophones
That sought to reproduce her tones.

Said Gus P. Sckunk to Al K. Sckum,
Seizing a wad of chewing-gum
Between his forefinger and thumb,
    And parking it discreetly:
"By Heck! We've spilt the beans! We're sunk!
We gotta scrap this vocal junk!
Say, Adelina," added Sckunk,
    Addressing Ada sweetly,
"You've been rechristened Adenoid!
You'd best go join the Unemployed!"

Last summer, just by chance, I went
To a cathedral town in Kent,
And sought (on light refreshment bent)
   "Ye Cosy Corner Tea-shoppe";
And there – ah, could it be her ghost? –
I saw a well-known form engrossed
In serving tepid buttered toast
   To a Colonial Bishop.*
Was this the Fricassée I knew,
Once more, alas! reduced to Stew?

How sad is glory in eclipse!
A question trembled on my lips,
And though a notice said "No Tips"
   (The tea-shop was Victorian),
I passed a silver coin across:
"Tell me about Los Angelos,"
I asked. She gave her head a toss
   While, like a true Gregorian,
The Bishop cried: "Excuse me, please!
Non Angelos sed Angeles!"

Moral

Though hard indeed may be the choice
'Twixt beauty and a lovely voice,
Each Cockney maiden must rejoice
   To read my tragic story,
To learn that there are gifts more rare
Than grace of form or features fair,
And though, maybe, her shingled hair
   Is woman's crowning glory,
Her chances can be much improved
By having adenoids removed!

*Beashop? – Pub.
More poetic licence. – H.G.

THE CRIES OF
— LONDON —

NO "Milk below maid" now awakes
The city with her plaintive pipe;
No tuneful pedlar hawks "Hot Cakes!"
No wench at dawn the silence breaks
   With strains of "Cherry Ripe!"
No cries of "Mack'rel!" subtly blend
With "Knives to grind!" or "Chairs to mend!"

The fireman's shout no more we hear;
   "Punch" and his satellites are dumb;
No more, when autumn days draw near,
Do songs of "Lavender!" rise clear
   Above the traffic's hum.
No "China orange" now is sold;
The muffin's knell is mutely toll'd!

And yet our nerves are sorely tried –
   Since Nature's lute has many a rift –
By "cries" which tube and 'bus provide:
"Fares please!" "'Old tight, miss!" "Full inside!"
   "No smoking in the lift!"

*

And oh! the gulf that separates
"Sweet lavender!" from "Mind the gates!"

THE POSTMAN AND
— THE LIFT —

" 'Most of our tenants pay rents of from £350 a year upward,'
says Mr Goddard, of Messrs Goddard and Smith, the well-
known Piccadilly house agents, 'and would strongly resent
having to ride up and down in lifts with postmen.' " – *Daily
Mail*.

I USED to live in Jermyn Street,
　Upon the seventh floor.
I occupied a charming suite,
Bed, bath, and boudoir, all complete;
　That flat is mine no more!
For in my lute appeared a rift:
They let the postman use the lift!

Was it for this I had to pay
　Three hundred pounds a year?
I never shall forget the day
A relative arrived to stay
　(First cousin to a peer);
My word! How Aunt Eliza sniff'd!
She met a postman in the lift!

"What!" she demanded, "must I ride
　With common men like him?"
She drew her scornful skirts aside,
Her smelling-bottle she applied,
　She shook in ev'ry limb.
"Be good enough," she said, "to sift
The lower orders from the lift!"

"Good Goddard! Fellow," I exclaimed,
   "Is there no public stair?
Are there no regulations framed
To make a working-man ashamed
   To breathe his betters' air?
To anarchy we surely drift
When common postmen use the lift!"

In vain I claim my legal rights,
   My landlord won't give way.
He says his pity it excites
To see men scaling seven flights
   So many times a day.
To other chambers I must shift,
Where postmen never use the lift!

THE VACUUM
— CLEANER —

A Poem of Progress

"Fond as I am of poetry," says Mrs Ella Wheeler Wilcox, the American poetess, "I can truly say that no epic ever impressed me so deeply, or so stirred my heart, as my first sight of a Vacuum Cleaner."

THOUGH Swinburne may sing like a siren,
    And Tennyson trill like a thrush,
Though bachelors rave about Byron,
    And girls over Longfellow gush,
No epic that critics can write of
    Supplies a delight that is keener
Than that which I daily obtain from the sight of
        A Vacuum Cleaner!

While lovers of music assemble
    Each night at the Opera House,
To shudder, to thrill, or to tremble
    At discords provided by Strauss,
Such orgies I savour the joys of,
    At home, 'mid surroundings serener,
Where daily I hear the Elektra-like noise of
        The Vacuum Cleaner!

The hedges with blossoms are laden,
　　The sunshine is bright up above,
And spring to the youth and the maiden
　　Gives promise of laughter and love;
While birds, more triumphantly singing,
　　In meadows and woods growing greener,
Announce to us elders that April is bringing
　　　The Vacuum Cleaner.

Though Time of "Old Masters" denude us,
　　Though strangers our treasures annex,
Though frauds and impostures delude us,
　　And counterfeits pain and perplex,
No fate that of Art would bereave us
　　Can ruffle our placid demeanour,
So long as Dame Fortune is willing to leave us
　　　The Vacuum Cleaner!

THE CRY OF THE
— ELDERS —

"With steady but increasing pace the world is approaching a point at which the cleverness of the young will amount to a social problem. Already things are getting uncomfortable for persons of age and sobriety, whose notion of happiness is to ruminate a few solid and simple ideas in freedom from disturbance." – *Macmillan's Magazine*.

O MY Children, do you hear your elders
      sighing?
  Do you wonder that senility should find
Your encyclopædic knowledge somewhat trying
     To the ordinary mind?
In the heyday of a former generation,
    Some respect for our intelligence was shown;
    And it's hard for us to cotton
    To the fact that *you've* forgotten
     More than *we* have ever known!

O my Children, do you hear your elders snoring,
    When the "chassis" of your motors you
      discuss?
Do you wonder that your "shop" is rather boring
     To such simple souls as us?*
Do you marvel that your dreary conversation
    Should evoke the yawns that "lie too deep for
    tears,"
    When you lecture to your betters
    About "tanks" and "carburettors,"
     About "sparking-plugs" and "gears"?

---

*"As us" is not grammar. – *Publisher's Reader*.
 "As we" is not verse. – *H.G.*

O my Little Ones, your parents were contented
    With an omnibus of two-horse pow'r alone,
In an epoch when the Underground was scented
      With a fragrance all its own.
Now the trains have doors that pinch us as we
      enter,
    And suspended to a strap we strive to stand;
    Or we nimbly board an "Arrow,"
    And our backbone turns to marrow,
      As we skid along the Strand!

O my Children, note the moral (like a kernel)
    I have hidden in the centre of my song!
Do not contradict a relative maternal,
      If she happens to be wrong!
Be indulgent to the author of your being;
    Never show him the contempt that you must
      feel;
    Treat him tolerantly, rather,
    Since a man who is *your* father
      Can't be wholly imbecile!

O my Children, we, the older generation,
    At whose feet you ought (in theory) to sit,
Are bewildered by your mental penetration,
      We are dazzled by your wit!
But we hopefully anticipate a future,
    When the airship shall replace the motor-'bus,
    And *your* children, when they meet you,
    Shall inevitably treat you
      Just as you are treating us!

— THE MOTRIOT —

After Robert Browning

IT was chickens, chickens, all the way,
  With children crossing the road like mad;
Police disguised in the hedgerows lay,
    Stop-watches and large white flags they had,
At nine o'clock o' this very day.

I broke the record to Tunbridge Wells,
    And I shouted aloud, to all concerned,
"Give room, good folk, do you hear my bells?"
    But my motor skidded and overturned;
Then exploded – and afterwards, what smells!

Alack! it was I rode over the son
    Of a butcher; rolled him all of a heap!
Nought man could do did I leave undone;
    And I thought that butcher's boys were cheap –
But this, poor man, 'twas his only one.

There's nobody in my motor now, –
    Just a tangled car in the ditch upset;
For the fun of the fair is, all allow,
    At the County Court, or, better yet,
By the very foot of the dock, I trow.

*

Thus I entered, and thus I go;
    In Court the magistrate sternly said,
"Five guineas fine, and the costs you owe!"
    I might not question, so promptly paid.
Henceforth I *walk*; I am safer so.

— TRAGEDY —

THAT morning, when my wife eloped
  With James, our chauffeur, how I moped!
What tragedies in life there are!
I'm dashed if I can start the car!

— IN-LAWS —

IT seems to me a crying shame
That humorists should all disparage
Those worthy persons whom we claim
   As relatives by marriage,
Who have been pilloried so long
In ev'ry so-called "comic" song
   That audiences never pause
   To think, but greet with loud guffaws
   All ribald jokes about "in-laws."

I always view with deep distress
   The rude and vulgar illustrations
In which the minor comic press
   Makes fun of those relations
Who stimulate the married life
Of many a happy man and wife,
   Whose constant presence should invest
   Existence with an added zest
   And make each union doubly blest.

I recollect, in days gone by,
    When courting my *inamorata*,
A backward, timid swain was I
    Who needed a self-starter:
And yet her people were so kind
They wouldn't let me change my mind;
    And though they knew I was no "catch"
    'Twas they who kept me to the scratch
    And practically *made* the match.

The mother of my *fiancée*
    (Who had six daughters then unmarried)
Would lightly laugh my qualms away,
    And all objections parried.
She pushed us in each other's arms,
And raved about her darling's charms,
    Making a comprehensive list
    (Including sev'ral that I'd missed)
    Till I no longer could resist.

As for my dear one's father, he
   Was just as tactful as her mother;
He'd always leave us, after tea,
   Alone with one another.
Locking the door, with some remark
About how "lovers love the dark,"
   He'd turn the gas off at the main;
   And I would sit for hours with Jane
   Trying to light the stove again.

My loved one's sisters (she had five)
   Behaved in as discreet a fashion,
And did their best to keep alive
   Our oft-times waning passion.
Before they entered any room
In which, amid sepulchral gloom,
   The chilly pair of lovers sat,
   They'd knock their loudest rat-a-tat
   Or cough outside upon the mat.

When first I set up house with Jane
    Her parents were of great assistance;
They never viewed me with disdain
    Or kept me at a distance.
Her father came, without a fuss,
Three nights a week, to dine with us;
    Her mother, with maternal zeal,
    Appeared at ev'ry other meal,
    And quite at home they made us feel.

They chose the carpets and the chintz,
    They bought the curtains (with our savings),
Replaced my set of Baxter prints
    With Marcus Stone engravings;
And ev'ry day, when we were out,
They'd move the furniture about
    And rearrange our little nest,
    And though at times we might protest,
    We knew, of course, that they knew best.

And when our tiny firstborn came
    Their loving-kindness quite nonplussed us
We'd chosen "Henry" as his name,
    But they preferred "Augustus":
And, later, though we'd wished to call
His sister "Mary" – not at all!
    In this we were allowed no voice,
    For they'd already made their choice,
    And she was duly christened "Joyce."

My wife has brothers, charming men,
   Who never seem to need inviting;
They know they're welcome in my den,
   And when I'm busy writing
They very often condescend
To sit with me for hours on end,
   Explaining how I'd make it pay
   By doing what I do to-day
   In some completely diff'rent way.

Their sisters, whom I love so well,
   Delight me with their girlish chatt'ring
They use my house as an hotel,
   Which is extremely flatt'ring.
It's really very nice to feel,
If *one* pops in to snatch a meal,
   Another's on the telephone;
   My wife and I are bound to own
   We're never lonely, or alone.

— BREAKFAST —

THE perfect breakfast, all must own,
Is that which man enjoys alone;
Peace, perfect peace, is found, they say,
Only with loved ones far away,
And there is naught but solitude
That suits the matutinal mood.

But there, alas! are tactless folk
Who choose that hour to jest and joke,
Whose conversation, brisk and bright,
Just bearable perhaps at night,
Fills with intolerable gloom
The self-respecting breakfast-room.
Thus, as I verily suspect,
Are many happy households wrecked;
So when you break your morning fast
Let no one share that first repast!

Dean Cope, the eminent divine,
Was breakfasting at half-past nine,
Perusing (as he munched his toast)
"The Anglican or Churchman's Post,"
When in there blew, to his distress,
The Bishop of the Diocese
(Most typical in size and girth
Of the Church Militant on Earth)
Who shouted "Cheerio, old chap!"
And gave the Dean a playful slap.

Alas! What ill-timed *bonhomie*!
The Dean inhaled his kedgeree,
And turning, with his face all black,
He slapped the breezy Bishop back!

Both lost their tempers there and then,
And in a trice these holy men
Began (with the most unholy zeal)
To throw the remnants of the meal
At one another! Buttered eggs

Bespattered aprons, gaitered legs
Were splashed with bacon; bits of sole
Fell thick on cassock, alb, and stole!
The dining-room became a sea
Of struggling Christianity,
And when at last the luckless Dean
Slipped on a pat of margarine,
The Bishop took a careful shot
And brained him with the mustard-pot!

A sight to make the angels weep!
How scandalized the local sheep
Who read descriptions of the scene
In ev'ry Parish Magazine!

The Diocese was deeply shocked;
The Dean, degraded and unfrocked,
Found refuge in a City slum,
Lay-reader to the Deaf and Dumb!

The Bishop lost his see, and sank
To rural Prebendary's rank!
No longer in his breezy way
He reads the Collect for the Day,
Or chants what proper hymns there be
For those of Riper Years at Sea!

At Matins and at Evensong
His cry goes up: "How long! How long!"
His groans are heard through aisle and apse
Bewailing his untimely lapse,
As he repents him of the crime
Of being bright at breakfast time!

FISH.

— BISHOP PROUT —

IN Burma, once, while Bishop Prout
Was preaching on Predestination,
There came a sudden waterspout
And drowned the congregation.
"O Heav'n!" cried he, "why can't you wait
Until they've handed round the plate!"

— THE TRAVELLER —

IN foreign travel one may find
A means to exercise the mind,
To broaden those parochial views
Which stay-at-homes so seldom lose
Until, with Baedeker in hand,
They leave their own, their native land.

A relative of mine, Aunt Maud,
For years had longed to go abroad;
She pined to breathe the ampler air
Of Schnitzelbad or Plage-sur-Mer;
She often felt that she would choke
If she remained at Basingstoke.

Alas! She could not ever rouse
Responsive feelings in her spouse
Who, when the subject was discussed,
Displayed no signs of "wanderlust";
"The air of Basingstoke," said he,
"Is plenty good enough for me!"

The strain at length became too great.
Encouraged by her daughter Kate,
Her husband's wishes she defied,
Turned (like a worm too sorely tried)
And, heedless of the nuptial yoke,
Shook off the dust of Basingstoke.

As when some parrot from the East,
By Fate from gilded cage released,
Will scarcely pause to wipe its mouth

Upon the perch ere hastening South,
So flew Aunt Maud, without delay,
And booked her passage to Bombay!

The Vicar begged her not to go,
Suggesting Aix-les-Bains or Pau
As better suited to her age
Than any land where tigers rage
And still grass-widows, one presumes,
Cremate themselves on husbands' tombs.

Unmoved, Aunt Maud declared that she
Must hold the gorgeous East in fee,
Must hear the sound of temple bells,
Must taste the joys, and smell the smells,
Of rickshaws, sweepers, and bazaars,
And tiffin 'neath the deodars!

She bought her outfit at the Stores:
A spear for sticking pigs (or boars),
A solar helmet, called *topee*,
Two punkahs and a puggaree;
An air-gun, too, because (with luck)
She hoped to bag a Bombay duck.

She ordered special underclothes
Of dungaree and cellulose,
A Jaeger sleeping-bag with flaps,
A rubber bath that would collapse,
And, since her figure was rotund,
She bought an "outsize" cummerbund.

So, in due course, she reached Bombay.
She'd meant to make a lengthy stay,
But, just within the week, alack!
A cable came to call her back,
Announcing that her daughter Kate
Proposed to wed a plumber's mate!

She hastened swiftly home, in time
To stop her offspring's social crime.
(The plumber chose another mate,
But rendered an "account to date,"
Including in his modest claim
"Man's time" and "Making good the same"!)

Back home in Basingstoke to-day,
Aunt Maud still dreams about Bombay.
She much surprised the local cow
By weaving garlands for its brow.
Her country-seat – it's called "The Pines" –
Is run on Anglo-Indian lines.

The Vicar, when he comes to dine,
Describes her curries as divine.
Her daughter Kate has found at last
A suitor of becoming caste –
She's got engaged to Lord St Barbe:
Half-witted, but a *pukka sahib*.

I love to hear Aunt Maud enlarge
On problems of the British Raj;
On questions that concern the East
Her talk is a perpetual feast;
And who so qualified to speak?
She's *lived* in India – for a week!

— IF...! —

I WENT to Murren (Switzerland)
For winter sports, you'll understand.
(I'm very fond of snow and ice,
Of alpenstocks and edelweiss.)
I booked my rooms at the hotel,
Unpacked, and, having rung the bell,

I asked the waiter would he please
To oil my skates and air my skis.
"Alas!" said he, "I greatly fear
You'll neither skate nor ski this year!
The thaw has melted ice and snow!
Now, if you'd come a year ago...!"

The sunny South of France I sought;
Blue goggles and a helmet bought;
Prepared to loiter, book in hand,
In sunshine, on a silver strand.

A blizzard blew, with rain and sleet;
The central heating wouldn't heat.
No form of fuel could I scrounge;
I sat and shivered in the lounge.
The natives all were forced to own
Such weather never had been known.
"It's quite exceptional," they said.
"Had you been here *last* year instead...!"

I went to Holland (Amsterdam),
For that's the sort of man I am,
To see the tulips in full bloom.
(They charged a fiver for my room!)
I met a p'liceman on the square,
And asked him could he tell me where
The flowers in serried masses grew
Of ev'ry size and shape and hue.
The fellow shook his head and sighed:
"The bulbs this season mostly died!
The frost," said he, "was so severe.
Now, if you'd only come *last* year...!"

I hastened off to far Japan,
Undaunted (I'm that type of man!),
For folks had told me how sublime
It was in cherry-blossom time.
But I had chosen, it appears,
The leanest, barrenest of years.
The cherry-crop had, if you please,
Been devastated by disease
And by – I can't recall the term –
Some strange exotic kind of worm!
'Twas quite abnormal, people swore;
Had I but come twelve months before...!

I hurried swiftly home, and went
To see a maiden aunt in Kent.
She welcomed me, and led me round
Her garden which is world-renowned.
We reached a border bleak and bare:
"I had such lovely larkspur there,
Less than a month ago!" she said.
"It's sad to think they're mostly dead.
And my delphiniums, too, I vow
Were wonderful! They're over now.
My columbines were quite unique!
If only you'd been here last week . . . !"

I fled – it seemed a kind of Fate –
To Worthing, to recuperate.
'Twas rumoured that at moments there
(Occasions happily most rare)
A pungent smell assailed the nose.
Like Aphrodite it arose
From out the sea, at change of tide:
A smell of sea-weed being fried,
Of rotting shell-fish and of slime –

I got it. I was just in time!

— CHANCE —

THOUGH most of us may disbelieve in
    fairies,
  And label Luck a superstitious myth,
If *we*'d had an experience like Mary's
  (I mean, of course, my cousin Mary Smith)
We certainly should realize, like her,
How oft the Unexpected *does* occur.

An aunt of hers, old Mrs Smith (of Barnet),
  Had given her a bracelet, subtly chased –
Two aluminium snakes with eyes of garnet
  Whose bodies were adroitly interlaced –
A bangle which poor Mary couldn't bear
But felt herself in duty bound to wear.

Last year she took her aunt off to the Lido,
  And there upon the sunny sands reclined
Or scudded through the waves like a torpedo –
  She looked so like one, too, from just behind –
While Mrs Smith sat by and viewed the scene
Or read the Barnet Parish Magazine.

One day, as Mary sported in the ocean,
  A shadow loomed beside her, slim and dark;
She heard a boatman cry, with deep emotion:
  "Guardati! Pesce cane!" ("Mind the shark!")
And, making headlong for the shore forthwith,
She sprang into the arms of Mrs Smith!

"Thank God you're safe!" said Auntie, fondly
    kissing
    Her niece's pallid cheek and anguished brow;
"But what is this, my child? Your bracelet's
    missing!
    You must have dropped it in the sea just now!
We can't allow that heirloom to be lost.
It must be found at once, whate'er the cost!"

"Perhaps the shark has swallowed it," said Mary.
    "If so," said Auntie, "he should be ashamed!
Send for the Doge! Where are the Bersaglieri?

What are the coastguards doing?" she
    exclaimed.
"With such a danger is there none to cope?
What's Mussolini there for, and the Pope?"

In vain did they employ the local diver
    And get the Doge to issue a decree
In which he offered anyone a fiver
    That bracelet to unearth – or to unsea!
Conscious at last that failure was complete,
They shook the spray of Venice off their feet.

This summer, Mrs Smith and cousin Mary
    Selected Westgate as a health-resort
Where bathing holds no risks for the unwary
    And shrimping is a well-protected sport,
And here they built their castles in the sand
And listened to the Borough Council Band.

One morning, on the pier where they were
    sitting,
    Said Mary: "What's that tune they've just
    encored?"
"That," said her aunt, "is the Refrain from
    Spitting –
    At least, it says so on the notice-board.
It's not an opera that I know well;
My favourite, of course, is *William Tell*."

Then, as she spoke, there came the sound of
    cheering,
    And see! along the asphalt esplanade
A noble army from the beach appearing
    Of man and boy, of matron and of maid,
And in their midst a giant fish they bore:

"A shark," they cried, "has just been washed
    ashore!"

At Mary's feet they laid the dead cetacean.*
  Her thoughts flew back to a Venetian bay
And, as they planned the beast's evisceration –
  I'll spare the lurid details, if I may –
She and her aunt exchanged a meaning glance
And prayed in secret to the god of Chance.

Poor Mrs Smith's excitement rose to fever,
  And Mary too grew anxious, I confess,
As someone slit the fish up with a cleaver
  And found within its vitals – can you guess?
You're wrong, alas! They didn't find a thing
Except two buttons and a piece of string!

Yes. Providence, performing many wonders,
  May move in a mysterious way, no doubt,
Yet will not always rectify our blunders,
  As Mrs Smith and Mary have found out.
The long arm of coincidence grows weak;
The skirts of happy chance are far to seek;
And Jonah's shark was probably unique.

*Sharks are not cetaceous. – *Pub*.
  This one was. – *H.G.*

— OPPORTUNITY —

WHEN Mrs Gorm (Aunt Eloïse)
　　Was stung to death by savage bees,
Her husband (Prebendary Gorm)
Put on his veil, and took the swarm.
He's publishing a book, next May,
On "How to Make Bee-keeping Pay."

— WASTE —

OUR governess – would you believe
It? – drowned herself on Christmas Eve!
This was a waste, as, anyway,
It would have been a holiday.

— THE BATH —

BROAD is the Gate and wide the Path
That leads man to his daily bath;
But ere you spend the shining hour
With plunge and spray, with sluice and show'r –
With all that teaches you to dread
The bath as little as your bed –
Remember, wheresoe'er you be,
To shut the door and turn the key!

I had a friend – my friend no more! –
Who failed to bolt his bath-room door;
A maiden aunt of his, one day,
Walked in, as half-submerged he lay!
She did not notice nephew John,
And turned the boiling water on!

He had no time, nor even scope,
To camouflage himself with soap,
But gave a yell and flung aside
The sponge 'neath which he sought to hide!
It fell to earth I know not where!
He beat his breast in his despair,

And then, like Venus from the foam,
Sprang into view, and made for home!

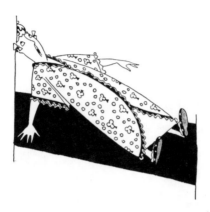

His aunt fell fainting to the ground!
Alas! they never brought her round!

She died, intestate, in her prime,
The victim of another's crime;
And John can never quite forget
How, by a breach of etiquette,
He lost, at one fell swoop (or plunge),
His aunt, his honour, and his sponge!

— THE DIRT CURE —

"Abandon Soap all ye who enter here!"

"I do not think cleanliness is to be recommended as an hygienic method.... The whole of the doctrine of fresh air requires to be revised.... There is no evidence that the man who does not take physical exercise is more liable to disease than the man who does." – Sir Almroth Wright.

TIME was when I gaily would wash myself
      daily;
  My body with soapsuds I polished;
Each morning I plotted to issue unspotted
  From baths (that have since been abolished).
But though I might lather and scrub with a will, I
Could never elude those confounded bacilli!

Time was when each casement, from attic to
      basement,
  Stood open all night to the breezes;
My molars might chatter, but what did that
      matter,
  Thought I, if I staved off diseases?
A practice so rigorous merely unstrung me,
And germs floated in at the window, and stung
      me!

Time was when I nightly would bicycle brightly
    Round Battersea Park, in a "sweater";
I felt that such vigour would strengthen my
      figure,
    And render my appetite better.
Alas! 'neath my cycling costume (call'd a "bike-
      robe")
I still was a prey to each virulent microbe!

The scientist's scathing indictment of bathing
    Has altered my methods completely.
I've given up coping with windows, or soaping;
    My sponges are packed away neatly.
My bicycle's sold, and I can't understand how
I ever attempted to emulate Sandow!

Unkempt and a sloven, in rooms like an oven,
    I lead a most healthy existence;
My stout epidermis so horny and firm is,
    Bacilli are kept at a distance.
No germ in my armour discovers a juncture;
My body no microbe is able to puncture!

— THE PEST —

I HATE the knave whose private life
　Is noted for its lack of morals,
Who starves his children, beats his wife,
　　Who fights and drinks and quarrels;
But oh! I view more sternly far
　　(How hostile grow my eyes of hazel!)
The rogue who suffers from catarrh –
　　The kind that's known as "nasal"!
With looks of loathing I behold
The wretched man who's got a cold!

Though criminals I can forgive,
　　And gladly suffer fools who bore me,
At peace with him I cannot live
　　Who scatters microbes o'er me!
He should be exiled, out of reach,
　　Condemned to dwell in isolation,
Who punctuates his ev'ry speech
　　With bouts of sternutation!
No blacker crime exists, I hold,
Than to transmit a heavy cold!

Then let me brand in harshest terms
  The caitiff who, in fashion stealthy,
Disseminates catarrhal germs
  Among the sane and healthy;
Who, when he ought to be in bed,
  Snorts like a pair of punctured bellows,
Until his fell complaint is spread
  Broadcast among his fellows!
With passion fierce and uncontrolled
I loathe the man who's got a cold!

CALCULATING
— CLARA —

O'ER the rugged mountain's brow
Clara threw the twins she nursed,
And remarked, "I wonder now
Which will reach the bottom first?"

— BABY —

BABY roused its father's ire,
By a cold and formal lisp,
So he placed it on the fire,
And reduced it to a crisp.
Mother said, "Oh, stop a bit!
This is *over*doing it!

— CANON GLOY —

ONE morning, just as Canon Gloy
   Was starting gaily for the station,
The Doctor said: "Your eldest boy
Must have another operation!"
"What!" cried the Canon. "Not again?
That's *twice* he's made me miss my train!"

— THE POET'S LIFE —

"A poet's life must almost necessarily be troubled," says Mr
Yeats. "If you could find a perfectly steady nature, you
would find a silent one."

HOW little does the public guess
The poet's fount of inspiration,
The dull despair, the storm and stress,
  The pain and tribulation,
The doleful days, the sleepless nights,
That darken ev'ry line he writes!

The noblest bards have all required
  A tragic source from which to borrow;
The choicest epics were inspired
  By some domestic sorrow,
I wrote my masterpiece that morning
When both the parlourmaids gave warning.

When from a window in Whitehall
  A flow'r-pot on my skull descended,
I penned those lines which nearly all
  The critics labelled "splendid";
That pot impinging on my cranium
Inspired my "Ode to a Geranium."

I wrote my "Ballad of Blue Blood,"
  So haunting, exquisite and tender,
The evening that my collar stud
  Rolled underneath the fender.
Were finer couplets ever written
By any man less sorely smitten?

— ENVOI —

BEHOLD how tenderly I treat
Each victim of my pen and brain,
And should I tread upon your feet,
    How lightly I leap off again;
Observe with what an airy grace
I fling my inkpot in your face!

To those whose intellect is small,
    This work should prove a priceless treasure;
To persons who have none at all,
    A never-ending fount of pleasure;
A mental stimulus or tonic
To all whose idiocy is chronic.

And you, my Readers (never mind
    Which category you come under),
Will, after due reflection, find
    My verse a constant source of wonder;
'Twill make you *think*, I dare to swear –
But *what* you think I do not care!

The verses in this book have been taken from the following sources:

ADAM'S APPLES
illustrated by John Reynolds (Methuen, 1930)
pp. 28-32, 111-15, 142-45

CANNED CLASSICS
illustrated by Lewis Baumer (Mills & Boon, 3rd edn., 1935)
*pp. 14-17, 18-19, 27, 58-59, 63-64, 83-84, 104-5, 117-18, 119-20,
152-53, 158*

DEPORTMENTAL DITTIES
illustrated by Lewis Baumer (Mills & Boon, n.d.)
pp. 48-50, 61-63, 79, 97

MISREPRESENTATIVE MEN
(Gay & Hancock, new and enlarged edn., 1910)
p. 159

MISREPRESENTATIVE WOMEN
illustrated by Dan Sayre Groesbeck (Edward Arnold, 1906)
pp. 76-78, 121-22

*MORE RUTHLESS RHYMES FOR HEARTLESS HOMES
illustrated by Ridgewell (Edward Arnold, 1930)
pp. 11, 25, 26 (bottom), 33, 45, 60, 90, 91, 124, 134, 146, 147, 157

THE MOTLEY MUSE
illustrated by Lewis Baumer (Edward Arnold, 1913)
pp. 40-41, 44, 46-47, 102-3, 106, 107-8, 116

RHYMES FOR RIPER YEARS
illustrated by Norah Brassey (Mills & Boon, 2nd edn., 1917)
pp. 73, 80-81, 82, 88-89, 109-10, 154-55

*RUTHLESS RHYMES FOR HEARTLESS HOMES
by Col. D. Streamer, illustrated by GH (Edward Arnold, 1899)
pp. 12 (both), 13, 26 (top), 43, 53, 65, 156 (both)

STRAINED RELATIONS
illustrated by H. Stuart Menzies and Hendy (Methuen, 1926)
pp. 20-24, 92-96, 125-29

VERSE AND WORSE
(Edward Arnold, 1905)
pp. 42-43, 123

THE WORLD'S WORKERS
illustrated by Fougasse (Methuen, 1928)
pp. 66-69, 135-38

THE WORLD WE LAUGH IN
illustrated by Fish (Methuen, 1924)
*pp. 34-35, 36-39, 51-53, 54-57, 70-72, 74-75, 85-87, 98-101, 130-33,
139-41, 149-51*

*All the verses from these two books have been most recently
republished as RUTHLESS RHYMES by Edward Arnold, 1984.